THE UNFINISHED ROAD

THE UNFINISHED ROAD

Jewish Survivors of Latvia Look Back

COLLECTED AND
EDITED BY

Gertrude Schneider

PRAEGER

New York
Westport, Connecticut
London

Library of Congress Cataloging-in-Publication Data

The Unfinished road : Jewish survivors of Latvia look back / collected
  and edited by Gertrude Schneider.
    p.   cm.
  Includes bibliographical references and index.
  ISBN 0–275–94093–4 (alk. paper)
  1. Holocaust, Jewish (1939–1945)—Latvia—Personal narratives.
  2. Jews—Latvia—Biography. I. Schneider, Gertrude.
DS135.R93L327 1991
940.53′08′094743—dc20   91–3343

British Library Cataloguing in Publication Data is available.

Library of Congress Catalog Card Number: 91–3343
ISBN: 0–275–94093–4

First published in 1991

Praeger Publishers, One Madison Avenue, New York, NY 10010
An imprint of Greenwood Publishing Group, Inc.

Printed in the United States of America

The paper used in this book complies with the
Permanent Paper Standard issued by the National
Information Standards Organization (Z39.48–1984).

10 9 8 7 6 5 4 3 2 1

Since this is the last book in a trilogy, I dedicate it to our third generation, meaning the grandchildren of the Jewish Survivors of Latvia.

I hope that just as they have been told of our plight by their parents, our beloved children, they will in turn tell their children and exhort them to continue in this way, so that each generation will remember what happened so long ago in the forests and fields of Latvia.

I further hope that our grandchildren realize what it meant to us, the survivors, to have children . . . it was an absolute act of faith! Despite our horrendous past, we went on with our lives almost as if we wanted to demonstrate that our own survival, in a small way, should indicate our triumph over the forces of evil.

As you grow older, you will understand all this much better. At this time I only ask that you carry on, both with our faith as well as with our memories!

Gertrude Schneider

Contents

MAP AND PHOTOGRAPHS FOLLOW PAGE 99.

Acknowledgments

I would like to thank the Research Foundation of the City University of New York for the grant given to me in 1990, which enabled me to bring to a close the extensive research needed for this work.

In Latvia and in Israel, two countries on this last itinerary, I was especially gratified to speak with several of the contributors to this volume and examine papers held by them. Special thanks also go the archivists in Riga and at Kibbutz Shefayim for being so helpful and well-prepared and to Liuba Rakhman and Isaac Leo Kram for their excellent translations.

To the staff at documentation centers in Warsaw and Gdańsk and at the former concentration camp Stutthof, now a museum and an archive, my deepest appreciation. It is only fair to say that I could never have succeeded in the research in Poland, had it not been for the superb translation and interpretation by my husband, Eric Schneider. The fact that he drove me to the many little villages where I could speak to witnesses played no small part in my piecing together the unbelievable events discussed in my story of Sophienwalde (Dziemiany).

Many thanks also to Dr. James T. Sabin, Executive Vice President of the Greenwood Publishing Group, and Mr. Mark Kane, the Production Editor. Both were always ready to listen and were extremely helpful in the final makeup of this volume.

Finally, I wish to thank the Executive Committee and the members of the Jewish Survivors of Latvia, who were supportive of my endeavors at all times. I could not have worked on this volume had it not been for the encouragement given to me by the president of the association, Steven Springfield, and the two vice presidents, Professors Howard Adelson and George Schwab. I am forever grateful.

1

The Unfinished Road

Gertrude Schneider

So as to gain access to the inhabitants of Dziemiany, formerly Sophienwalde, I sought out the priest of the village and asked him to help me. With my husband Eric as my interpreter, I told him that I was doing research on satellite camps of Stutthof. Father Ireneusz Lehmann was very kind. "Of course I will help you," he said. "I will introduce you to many of the old people here. They remember the camp. Then, when you are finished," he added, "you must come to my house at Number One, Ulica Robotnicza, the Street of the Workers, for it is at my house where the road ends. . . . those Jewish women never finished it."

Dziemiany is a sleepy little village, situated between Chojnice and Gdańsk. It is a pretty place, with its picturesque lake, its old-fashioned railroad station, and its beautiful church. It boasts of an old stone quarry and there is a large lumberyard near the railroad station, where many of Dziemiany's citizens work. Most live in small, well-kept houses; some of them keep a few chickens, others keep bees, there are bicycles and motorcycles, and even a few cars.

There are also some red brick buildings which do not quite fit into these surroundings. They are former SS barracks, but they are now inhabited by citizens of Dziemiany. To all appearances, Dziemiany is an inconspicuous place, curiously remote and quiet, just as are many other villages in that part of Poland. Yet, there is a sinister aspect . . .

In 1944, Dziemiany was called Sophienwalde and it was to be part of a tremendous project called Polygon, to be administered by *Obersturmbannfuehrer* Otto Neubauer. It existed on a master plan designed by German architects on orders from the *Reichsfuehrer* SS, Heinrich Himmler. Polygon was to encompass an area of over five hundred square kilometers, where only Germans would be permitted to reside. It was to be a place for training and maneuvers, both for SS and Army. In the extensive correspondence between Himmler and Oswald Pohl, the man in charge of economic development involving concentration camp labor and loot, it was established that the erection of army and SS barracks and the building of a new road was the first priority.

Materials for this grandiose plan were within reach. The stone quarry and the abundant lumber were right there, in Sophienwalde. Bricks would be manufactured in Bruss, now Bruzy, just ten kilometers south of Sophienwalde. And as to workers—ah yes, they, too, were within reach. There was a camp containing two hundred Dutchmen who had been sent to the Reich for labor, there was a settlement consisting of five hundred evacuees from Warsaw as well as some fifty men and women brought from another such settlement in Potulice, and last, but not least, only thirty-five kilometers east of Gdańsk and thus within reach, there was an infamous concentration and extermination camp Stutthof, where the Germans could get the cheapest labor of all: They could get and did get Jewish women.

During that summer of 1944, Stutthof was bursting at its seams. It had originally been a concentration camp mainly for Poles, but circumstances such as a shrinking frontline and an excess of prisoners at Auschwitz and other such places transformed it into an extermination camp. A separate section for Jews was added, complete with sick bay and a small gas chamber. The existing crematorium was enlarged, but even so, it never proved to be efficient enough.

Although the gas chamber was a small one, as gas chambers go, it could nevertheless "dispatch" between fifty and sixty Jews every thirty minutes. Since it did work around the clock, with the victims standing right beside it awaiting their end, there were just too many bodies to be burned, even with the new crematorium.

To remedy this untenable situation, prisoners dug several large ditches right next to the Jewish camp, and these ditches were used for burning the overflow of corpses. The stench of this on-going operation was evident long before the camp came into view.

On the other hand, when approaching it from the main road, it looked promising. The long, low-slung white buildings had green shutters, there were beautiful flowers all around these buildings, and the grass was lush and green.

To be sure, it was a clever ploy. Yet, we, the remnants of Latvian and German Jews, experienced prisoners though we were, felt strangely comforted by the looks of the camp. After having been transported across the Baltic Sea and then down the Vistula to the village of Stutthof, we were hungry, quite dirty, terribly thirsty, and we waited impatiently on the sparse meadow in front of the gate to be admitted.

We had left Riga, the capital of Latvia, late Sunday morning, August 6, 1944, on the vessel *Bremerhafen*. There were almost two thousand of us—eleven hundred men and nine hundred women. There were also over three thousand Hungarian Jewish women, who had arrived in Riga only three months earlier, via Auschwitz. In addition, there were almost three thousand Russian prisoners of war.

Another transport of Jews was to come later, at the end of September, and that would make the city of Riga *judenrein* (cleansed of Jews).

Our journey on the *Bremerhafen* had lasted two days and two nights, but since we were crowded in the hold, as well as hot, hungry, and thirsty, the voyage seemed much longer.

The crew consisted of Austrian soldiers. It was disheartening to see that they were still what they had always been: Anti-Semites of the worst sort! When we attempted to go up on deck, where portable latrines had been set up, it was they who made it difficult. While they did not beat us, their disdain and dislike was obvious and insulting. Even the most naive among the prisoners realized that the war would not and could not last much longer. Yet, those Austrian soldiers, who had far more access to news, evidently still believed in Germany's victory.

The *Bremerhafen* docked at Danzig (Gdańsk) before noon, on Tuesday, August 8. The SS herded us onto a large meadow, where each person received a small loaf of bread; there were several locations where water was available from large pitchers. Thus, we recuperated somewhat from the stress of our voyage. Although there was a tiny stream in the meadow, which divided us from the men, we were able to speak to one another and try to bolster each others' morale.

We were depressed. Even the optimists among us were unhappy, since we had been taken away from Riga just as the frontline advanced toward the city. With our hopes of liberation dashed, we now had to face the uncertainty of our existence once more. We had no idea that of the eleven hundred men no more than three hundred would live to see freedom. Of the nine hundred women, however, almost five hundred survived the war, but over sixty died shortly after liberation; they died with the knowledge that the Thousand Year Reich had been vanquished.

Curiously, of the subsequent transport from Riga, which contained seven hundred men and one thousand women, Latvian, Lithuanian, and German Jews, over five hundred men survived, but only two hundred women did so.

On that eighth day of August 1944, while we were apprehensive of what the immediate future would have in store for us, we were more than certain that the war would soon be over, and we fervently hoped that we would survive.

All too soon, with the setting of the sun, we had to bid farewell to our men and the SS ordered us onto barges, which were connected by chains. What followed was a horrible night in the stinking, slimy holds of these barges, without water, without toilets, suffering from seasickness brought on by the vile smells and the movement of the barges on the unruly waves of the Vistula.

We arrived at the small town of Stutthof in a sorry state. How this one night had changed us! How awful we smelled! How grimy we looked! How incongruous we seemed when compared to the clean inhabitants of the town! And how disdainful and nauseated they looked at us . . .

We formed columns, five women to each row, and marched on old-fashioned cobblestones to the camp. The men were unloaded after us and were directed to the other half of the large, grassy plaza in front of the camp's iron gate.

After what seemed an eternity, we were given water, brought out by inmates. They managed to warn the older women about the "cut-off" age of forty. In fact, they may have saved many lives, since nearly all the women over forty (including my mother, Charlotte Hirschhorn, who was forty-six at the time) made themselves a few years younger when we were finally admitted, registered, and given new numbers. Also in accordance with what the inmates had told us, the handful of youngsters still alive among us, made themselves older, to be at at least fourteen. My sister, Rita, did so, too.

That first night in Stutthof was spent in Block 5. It was meant to accommodate perhaps three hundred women, and we were nine hundred. In charge of us was Maks Murolf, a Pole called "the terror of Stutthof," who sported the red triangle of the political prisoner. He beat us with such abandon and cruelty that his frequent, unexpected appearances were enough to induce panic. At day's end, as we were given some undefinable soup, Maks bloodied several of the new arrivals to such an extent that they were selected for the gas chamber only two days later. He did the same thing to the Hungarian women, who were in the two blocks on either side of us. At least fifty of them were among those selected for extermination.

By that time, we had already been taken to blocks 19, 20, 21, and 22, in the Jewish part of the camp. At this, our first selection in Stutthof, we had to undress completely, were told to make a bundle of our clothes and shoes, and while carrying the bundle, walk between several SS men, one of them with bright red hair, wearing a white coat. He stopped my beautiful sister and asked her "How old are you?" When she replied "I am seventeen, *Herr Doktor*," he said, with a grin, "You are well-developed!" and let her pass. Little did he know that she was weeks short of her fourteenth birthday! We blessed the inmates who had given us the timely warning!

From time to time, one of the other SS men asked to see what was in a bundle. He needed not to have bothered. When we were transferred from Block 5 to the Jewish camp, Maks beat us so severely that we left behind almost every item we had brought with us from Riga, in some cases even our spoons.

My mother, my sister, and I were in Block 19. Sixty women were selected from among us and taken away immediately. During the next few days we were joined by women who had come from Auschwitz; their stories were incredible.

On August 13, the majority of our men were seen leaving. Rumors had it that they were being transferred to Buchenwald. We were heartbroken. The Russian prisoners, who brought our food, managed to smuggle in some letters. We got one too, on a tiny piece of paper. In his beautiful handwriting, my father, Pinkas Hirschhorn, wrote: *"Behuetet einander. Kopf hoch, nicht aufgeben, es dauert nicht mehr lange. Wir treffen uns in Wien!"* (Take care of each other. Keep your heads high, don't give up, it won't take long anymore. We'll meet again in Vienna!) Alas, it was not to be.

On August 17, there was another selection, done in a different manner, during roll call. One hundred women were "chosen" and taken into the next block, which had been emptied the day before. Half of the hundred were from our transport, among them Elizabeth Weiss, mother of my friend Hertha, and Leah Granierer, mother of my friend Leo, both Viennese. Since, unknown to the Germans, the barbed wire between blocks 19 and 20 was loose on the bottom, during the night thirty-eight women, including Weiss and Granierer, crawled under the wire and came back to us.

Morning roll call . . . the women were counted . . . the SS women and the Ukrainian Block Elder became hysterical. They looked into every face and eventually selected not thirty-eight, but seventy-six instead . . . as a punishment. The Ukrainian asked my mother "Where were you, old one?" My mother answered in Russian *"Ya Tuda Byla"* (I was here) and in that way, thinking fast and depending on her language talent, saved her life and certainly that of my sister and mine. As for Elizabeth Weiss and Leah Granierer, neither one was singled out or questioned, and both managed to survive the war!

The 138 women were gassed during that same day. We actually saw them walk away, in the direction of the smoking chimney. The gas chamber and the crematorium were next to each other. We now understood and believed the stories told to us by the women who had come from Auschwitz. Just a few years earlier, it had taken us quite a long time to believe the rumors of mass graves in the forests around Riga. We had come a long way since Rumbuli and Bikerniek and we learned the truth about the gas chamber and the crematorium of Stutthof very soon.

More women who had gone through Auschwitz were added to the blocks. Some were from Lodz, from Kraków, from Warsaw. It was very crowded and many of us slept outside, on the sandy soil. The stories we told each other were more or less the same . . . ghettos, camps, hunger, uncertainty, loss of loved ones, attempts at resistance, and failure. It seemed that we were doomed; yet there were songs, sad and wistful, there was poetry, and that helped us to forget the hunger and the vermin plaguing us.

On Sunday, August 19, five tables were set up in front of the blocks and we were told that several thousand women were to be sent to work outside Stutthof. Each registrar wrote down about a thousand numbers, no names, just numbers. Not having names was the least of our worries.

Five days later, on August 24, the numbers of five hundred women were called. My mother and sister were among them. I was not. It seemed that I had been registered by another person and was not part of their sequence.

A Polish Jewess, also on a different list from that of her daughter, had the idea to simply change dresses and thus numbers, since we wore the numbers sewn on our prison garb. I was too stupid or maybe too scared to follow her advice. I believe I was in shock. First my father, and now my mother and sister. It was too much. I could not even cry. My mother begged the registrars, she begged the SS women, she went down on her knees in front of Maks Murolf . . . nothing helped. The five hundred women left for an unknown destination and I was alone.

They were taken to the railroad station in the town of Stutthof and after several hours' ride arrived in Sophienwalde. Before leaving the camp, each woman had received a blanket and a double ration of bread. In Sophienwalde their new accommodations consisted of small huts, just big enough for fifteen women to lie on the ground next to each other. Each hut had a tiny little window. The camp had one large latrine for the women, but there was no place to get washed. There was the ubiquitous barbed wire, and there were four towers for the guards. In front of the gate leading into the camp, there was a large barrack, made up of three sections, one containing an apartment for the *Kommandant* as well as rooms for three SS women, Charlotte Rose, Erika Loescher, and Martha Mueller. The second section housed the fourteen guards and their *Unterscharfuehrer*, and the middle section held a large kitchen. Next to the gate was a pump, the only place where water was available. It was used mainly to fill the kettles for soup, and for the personal needs of the SS men and women.

The *Kommandant* was *Sturmscharfuehrer* Willi Schultz. His first act of office was to choose several women for kitchen duty. Head cook was to be Bertl Schwartz, who had held that same position at the model farm Jungfernhof near Riga. As Camp Elder Schultz appointed a young Hungarian, Resi Goldstein; her two assistants were also Hungarian. (Almost two thirds of the women were Hungarian.) He then chose several *Kapos* for the various work details, called *Kommandos*.

Schultz explained that roads would be built as well as brick barracks, that bricks would have to be unloaded, that lumber was to be carried to wherever needed, and that the work was to be done as efficiently as possible. What he did not say was that it had to be accomplished on a minimum of food.

Poles, or as they were now known *"Volksdeutsche,"* from the village and surroundings would be the supervisors and were to be addressed as *Meister*. The most difficult job would be roofing, and that would be administered by *Firma* Zemke. It seemed that several barracks had already been started to be built by Polish laborers, but the roofs were to be installed by women. Schultz chose ten "roofers," all quite young, all Hungarian.

Among the fifteen women in the hut where my mother and sister lived were three Hungarian girls, and one of them was part of the roofing crew. Although she did not look it, she was a sick girl. As the first few days went by, she became visibly weaker and the job became too much for her. Only three weeks after her arrival in Sophienwalde, on a cool, rainy September day, she slipped from the high ladder, fell onto a ledge, and broke her neck.

When the *Kommandos* came home that evening, my mother and sister, both of whom worked at one of the road building outfits administered by *Firma* Hain, found out about the tragedy. After comforting the two friends of the dead girl, my mother left the hut and asked the guard at the gate to let her see the *Kommandant*.

(Any survivor who reads this will realize how unorthodox and dangerous such a request was in that place and at that time. On the other hand, anyone who knew my indomitable, clever mother only remotely will not only marvel at her audacity, but will not be too surprised. . . . only she would have dared to do such a thing!)

Just as the guard tried to chase her away, *Sturmscharfuehrer* Schultz came down the steps from the kitchen. He must have heard the commotion, for he asked her why she wanted to see him. My mother told him of having left behind a daughter in Stutthof, who was an accomplished roofer! Now, with this poor Hungarian girl having died, would he perhaps ask the main camp to send "such a much needed expert" to Sophienwalde? He asked when and where this daughter had learned such a skill. My mother, lying through her teeth, told him that I had done so while in the ghetto of Riga and later at the concentration camp Kaiserwald.

Thoughtfully, Schultz asked her for my number. That part was easy, since our numbers were consecutive: My number, 61,811, was first; my mother's number, 61,812, was next, and last was my sister Rita's, number 61,813. He promised to do whatever he could and she went back into the hut, not telling anyone, not even my sister, what she had done. She was superstitious and did not want to talk about her scheme, fearing it would go awry.

In the meantime, those three lonely weeks in Stutthof had taken their toll on me. Many of the women who had come with us from Riga had left Stutthof for outside camps. One big transport called *Baugruppe Weichsel* was also joining the Polygon project. One thousand women were part of it and although I must have been on one of the lists, my number was never called. In addition to large transports, quite a few women were sent out to help farmers in the vicinity bring in the harvest. Most of the women were volunteers, but even when the SS did the choosing, I was deemed too skinny or perhaps, wearing eyeglasses, not the right type for farm work. I was quite shaken when Alice Brunn left—she had been on the same train with us when we left Vienna in February of 1942, to go "East for Resettlement." Another Viennese, Selma Breitner, left too. She had admonished me several times in the last few days to wash myself. I just did not care anymore.

Also during that time, there were two selections in Block 19. At the first one, on August 27, Sophie Barsam was chosen; the clothing store in Vienna where she had worked before Hitler took Austria in March of 1938 had been just around the corner from where my grandparents had a restaurant, and although she was still a young woman, she looked a little like my pretty grandmother.

After her number had been entered on the list, which meant that she was slated to go to the gas chamber on the next day, she came to me and said that the Ukrainian block elder had promised to "erase" her number from the death list, if she could give her something of value. I had my father's signet ring in my shoe and I gave it to her. She then stayed with me for the next nine days but was again put on the list on September 5, the day of the subsequent selection, and was sent to the gas the very next day. By that time, she did not care anymore either. She was only glad that her husband, an Armenian, had died so young and that her two boys had gone to England with a children's transport in 1939. She blessed me before she left. He total resignation to her fate broke my heart.

On September 9, we had a great "delousing" procedure. For several hours we stood stark naked in front of the barracks, while our infested clothes were dipped into a foul-smelling solution. From there they wandered into a hot air contraption. The heat seemed to revive the lice instead of killing them. From standing in the cold, damp air, however, a number of women got sick and were taken to the *Revier,* the useless sick bay. I worked there for a few days, before the delousing procedure, cleaning the floors. From the sick bay I saw several small groups, sometimes men and sometimes women, being taken to the gas chamber. All of the victims were Jewish.

The rear of our barrack now housed a number of gypsies. They were quite colorful, they sang, they were in much better shape than we were, and many of them were openly anti-Semitic and called us names. Yet, one of them insisted on telling me what the future would hold in store for me. Despite my unwillingness to listen, she took my hand and predicted, among other things—all of which came true—that I would see "some" of my loved ones again. She also taught me a few Romany words and some Hungarian songs.

On September 16, during the interminable morning roll call, my number was called. The blood literally froze in my veins and I could not move. Luckily, the girl next to me pushed me forward. With a show of impatience, the SS woman motioned for me to follow her. I could see that she found me utterly disgusting in my rumpled, dirty "zebra" dress, without socks or stockings, with my thin legs sticking out of the good old army shoes I wore, a reminder of the German Airforce *Kommando* where I had worked in Riga. To top it off, I also had a string tied around my waist on which hung a battered enamel dish.

Shaking with fear, I followed her. When I realized that we were not going in the direction of the gas chamber and crematorium, I started to hope for all kinds of miracles and I thought of the gypsy.

At the gate through which we had first entered Stutthof, I was told to wait. After a while, a Polish prisoner came out of the administration building and handed me a piece of bread and a blanket. He winked at me. That evening, when I unfolded the blanket, I found that he had put in a set of extra prison underwear—a truly magnificent gift!

A guard appeared from another building, and the two of us walked to the town of Stutthof. Again there was a wait and then we boarded the train which consisted of open cattle cars. During all this time, he never said a word to me. As the train started moving, I ate my bread— all of it—just like a real experienced concentration camp prisoner. He shook his head disdainfully but did not say anything. I looked at the beautiful fields we passed; people were bringing in the harvest and I tried to guess whether any of the girls who had left the camp were among the workers.

It was almost evening when we arrived at a station with a sign "Sophienwalde." The silent guard motioned for me to jump down from the train. We walked a distance of perhaps a hundred yards and the familiar outline of a camp, barbed wire and watchtowers, came into sight. Only the little huts were unusual.

Inside the camp, several women were milling around. Suddenly, a tall, immaculate officer came down the steps of the barrack outside the gate. My guard stood at attention, reported that he had brought prisoner number 61,811 as ordered, and pointed to me in a rather disgusted manner. The officer—it was Schultz, of course, though I did not know it just then—looked at this absolutely repelling, emaciated, and dirty apparition, put his hands on his hips, and said in an incredulous tone, *"Du bist der Dachdecker?"* (You are the roofer?) At that same moment, I thought I saw my sister among the women at the gate. Thus, with a mixture of trepidation and bravado I answered, *"Jawohl, Herr*

Kommandant.'' His next words were the nicest ones I ever heard in all my life: "Go to your mother; she will take care of you!''

It had indeed been my sister at the fence; to this day she does not know what made her go there. She watched the guard and Schultz and thought she was dreaming when she recognized me . . . I walked through the gate, she took my hand and brought me into Hut 3, to our mother. Both of them cleaned me up; then mother told me what kind of work I would have to do.

Early next morning, when climbing up the ladder to my first roof, I found myself alone. The other nine roofers were busy at other sites. I had hoped to copy what they were doing. Examining the pot of tar mixed with cement and the shell-shaped bricks, I told the *Meister* that I had worked with totally different materials in Riga and asked him to show me how it was done here. To my amazement, I did a very credible job . . . my roof is still there, in Dziemiany, and the people living in that former barrack told me that it never leaks! At any rate, Schultz was so pleased by the *Meister's* report that he gave my mother an extra piece of bread for me that very evening.

The following day we worked only until noon. In the afternoon all five hundred of us were taken to the lake and had to bathe in it. This was done every third day. My sister told me that it had been great fun at first, but now it started to get cold and proved to be rather unpleasant. Luckily, after October 1 the bathing in the lake was discontinued—it was easier to stay dirty than to freeze to death.

That first week in October, each woman received a pair of long, male underwear and a tattered coat. I found the letters with which Schultz had bombarded Stutthof at the time, requesting warm clothing for the sake of greater efficiency. Now his request had been granted. Our three coats were black; my mother considered it a bad omen in regard to ever seeing father again. She was right.

Rations in Sophienwalde were the same as in Stutthof. Since the work was extremely taxing, however, we suffered from constant hunger, got progressively weaker, and many got ill. On October 24, our two physicians, Dr. Stein from Vienna and Dr. Loewy from Košice, Czechoslovakia, were told to assemble their worst cases and did so. Thirty-five women were sent away that evening. We thought they had been sent to Stutthof, but we were wrong.

In exchange for these sick women, we received thirty-five healthy women, among them several who had come from Riga to Stutthof with the second transport, arriving there on October 1. They told us about an

outbreak of spotted typhoid fever at the main camp and soon after their
arrival, the epidemic struck our camp as well. One mother from Libau
(Liepaja) lost her daughter; two young women from Vilno (Vilnius) died,
and so did three girls from Germany, and three of the Hungarians. They
were buried in Lesno, a small village near Sophienwalde. We were down
to 489 women.

The two doctors now had two full huts of patients; each contained
twenty "beds," in two layers, with the lower beds only inches from the
floor and the upper bunk about three feet above, so that it was impossible to sit up. The patients could not have done so anyway.

When there were no more roofs to be done, I worked at other *Kommandos*. Once I went to the railroad to unload bricks. On the way there,
I had an unpleasant shock. A detachment of Latvian SS walked straight
toward us and in the first row was a well-known, redheaded guard from
Kaiserwald, singing the Latvian song *"Cel Mani Par, Par Daugavu"*
("Take Me Across the Daugava River"). I was certain that he had recognized me, just as I had recognized him, for he had often chased me
away from the barbed wire fence when I talked to my father or to boys
who were my friends.

I was quite upset by his presence here in Sophienwalde, and I was
afraid. All of us knew by now that the Latvian SS men were worse than
any of the other groups that maltreated us. His name was Vilis Kruze.

What I did not know at the time and first found out when I did research in Riga, in the archives of Stutthof, and in speaking to witnesses in Dziemiany in these last few years, was the fact that Kruze at
that time was one of seventy medical students, housed in the same red
brick buildings that we and some Polish laborers had erected and com-
pleted. We had wondered why they had to have troughs on both sides
of the stone floor in one of the buildings. . . . and I only learned their
purpose four decades after the fact! They were dissecting cadavers while
learning human anatomy, and it was those seventy would-be doctors
who had received the thirty-five women from our camp! One body per
two students!

The Pole, Włødzimirz Markuszewski, who had to carry out the dis-
sected cadavers in large baskets nearly lost his mind. He survived and
we met in his native Warsaw in January of 1990. I recognized him
immediately as one of the workers whom I had known at the time.

I also found out from one of the Jewish survivors of Sophienwalde,
Hertha Weiss, that she had come back to the camp very late on that
night, had seen the van still standing in front of the gate, and had heard
the moans of the people in it. Evidently, the authorities waited for com-

plete darkness to deliver the unfortunate victims to the red brick building, which was not too far away, but not in the direction of the railroad station. I also looked at the entry roster in Stutthof for that day and the next. There aren't any.

Very often, especially when the weather was bad, the roofers had to help the other women on the all-important road. Four girls usually serviced a lorry and wherever needed, we were added. Whenever my strength gave out—and it happened from time to time—either my mother or my sister came over to help me do my share of filling the lorry, so that the other three women would not be at odds with me. While the work was physically much harder than roofing, it was neither as dangerous nor as lonely. I got to know many of the girls well and listened to their stories with great interest. Each story was somehow different.

There was Gerda Rose, a judge's daughter from Hamburg, blond and blue-eyed, there was Hannelore Kahn, there was Fritzi Kohn, a native of Austria's beautiful Burgenland, there was big, strong Chasia Warschafski from Vilno, who could fill the lorry single-handedly, there was Terry Weissmann from Sighet, who taught me many haunting Hungarian ballads, and there was Liuba Goldmann from Lodz, who told us about that Polish ghetto and what had happened to the Jews who had been sent there from Germany and Austria. They had been the first to die.

My knowledge of Polish hit songs comes from Liuba. She had quite a repertoire, but her voice was not that great. I had to entertain the crew by usually singing songs whose words I barely understood. Eventually, I learned that too, but in the meantime I was just like a parrot.

In November my sister developed an enormous boil on her right foot. She could not get into her shoe. We were quite desperate. My mother took the second pair of underwear that I had been given in Stutthof and bartered it for a brown, smelly ointment, which proved to be the proper medication for the boil. Once again, she had taken a chance because of one of her children. She had left the road on which she toiled and had run across a field into a house where she had seen a woman. The danger of being caught did not deter her.

The inhabitants of Sophienwalde, mainly *Volksdeutsche,* who spoke German with a Polish accent and Polish with a German accent, did some business with the inmates of the Dutch and British camps and also with the small contingent of Italian prisoners. These lucky men received packages from home. We, on the other hand, were destitute and so they had only very few dealings with us. In addition, we were constantly watched by our SS guards, even though they must have known that we had nowhere to go. At any rate, they were always more ferocious than the *Wehrmacht* guards.

A group of us, myself included, were now busy building a large brick house, partially underground, which was to replace our little huts and become our new camp. Each room in the house was to hold fifty women, with three layers of bunks so close to each other that it was impossible to sit up. It was to be ready by January 1, 1945, but there were delays.

Now the bitter cold became the real enemy. Each hut had a tiny stove, but most of the time there was little wood. The road now extended almost up to the forest and the women who built that part of it came home carrying twigs. That was not very safe to do, however, for several women, among them Gittel Abramowitz of Vilno, were shot and killed by trigger-happy guards for carrying too much wood.

On December 15, Schultz received visitors. His wife and two little girls—we were not sure that both were his daughters—came for a week and were then to go with him for a well-earned Christmas vacation. These news of him were of great importance to us. It was all so glamorous. Since the maid was one of our own, we were well informed of his doings. We were scandalized by the fact that Schultz had been carrying on with one of the SS women, Erika, and since we knew that she was pregnant, we wondered how he would handle the dilemma. We never did find out.

While Martha and Lotte rarely interfered with our camp elder, Erika could be mischievous and even cruel at times. Yet, she had a soft spot for my mother. She once showed us a picture of her own mother, and we were struck by the uncanny resemblance. On such a little thing hinged our eventual survival!

Schultz and family left on December 19. The camp, now numbering 488 women, was to be administered by an *Obersturmfuehrer* sent from Stutthof, for the next four weeks.

That same day, my mother collapsed on the road and with the help of Chayele Rozenthal from Vilno, my sister carried her to the sick bay. Dr. Stein diagnosed pneumonia.

I had been at the new construction site, working on the roof. When I came home and heard what had happened, I ran to the sick bay but the Slovakian physician did not want to let me come in. Almost crazy with worry, I pushed her aside and entered the hut, where I found my delirious mother sharing a bunk with a woman who had spotted typhoid fever. Yet, there were other bunks, with only one person in them, and I protested vehemently. The doctor was quite angry. She said, among other things, that ''most children had lost their mothers already some time ago." I then asked her bitterly whether the death of my mother would help those others, and I was so upset that I turned my back on her and put my cold hands on my poor mother's burning forehead. There was little else I could do.

Dr. Stein came in from the other hut. After talking to Dr. Loewy, she told me that I had made an enemy of her colleague by insulting her. At her urging and for my mother's sake I begged the doctor's forgiveness. However, Dr. Loewy did not take my proffered hand, thus not accepting my apology. Her enmity was to have dire consequences and almost cost us our lives.

I came back to Hut 3 shaken and desperate. This state lasted for my sister and me for ten days, until my mother's fever broke. She was extremely weak and had a persistent, hacking cough, but when she saw us, she smiled. She could not eat solids and so Rita and I made do with one soup between us, giving the other soup to mother. Little by little, she could eat pieces of bread soaked in soup; Rita and I ate the crusts. The woman next to her, a friend of the camp elder, sometimes got extra rations. She gave mother some bread for us because, as she said, "You have such good children!"

By January 4, 1945, parts of the new building were ready. The sick were the first to be housed there. They were transferred by being loaded onto little wagons, drawn by horses. There were sixty-one patients; we counted them. The rest of us still remained in the ice-cold huts, but now both Rita and I were part of the new building's work detail, and so we could visit our mother every day, at least for a few minutes.

On January 10, I asked to see Resi Goldstein. I told her that January 11 was my parents' silver anniversary—would she permit my sister and me to pump the water for the whole camp's soup and give me some bread, margarine, and a carrot for it? I told her that I would fashion a "cake" from these ingredients and would bring it to my mother's sickbed. Goldstein was a coarse young woman, but she had a human side and was intrigued. She agreed to the bargain. In fact, after we had pumped water for two hours, she let us go and added a little bag of sugar to our "wages." I made a heart from one piece of bread; it rested on a regular slice. The margarine acted like buttercream and from the cut-up carrot I fashioned a "25." The whole thing was enhanced by the unexpected, precious sugar. Rita and I brought the cake to Mama and she was very pleased by what we had done. She cried. Our thoughts were with our father.

Finally, the new building was ready and the camp was moved to it, albeit in stages. Since our mother was already there, and since we were in Hut 3, we managed to be among the first to be transferred. We had to walk, but since we had very little to carry, it was not too bad. It was not too far and for the rest of our stay in Sophienwalde, we had to come back to the old camp in order to get our soup. The new building never had a kitchen. (According to the "old" inhabitants of Sophienwalde, it collapsed in 1946.)

On January 25, mother was discharged from sick bay and joined us in our new bunks. She was made part of the cleaning detail.

Once, while standing in line at the old camp and waiting for my soup, I called out to my sister that I was going to unload bricks and would be back late. Just then, unnoticed by me, the substitute *Kommandant* walked by. Recognizing my Viennese accent, he talked to me and said that he had been in Vienna and that it was a beautiful city. He mentioned that Schultz was to be back in two or three days and that he, on the other hand, was due back at Stutthof and would go from there to Buchenwald. I could not restrain myself from telling him about my father's presumable presence there. In fact, I asked him to find my father and tell him that we were alive and well. From the man's demeanor I could tell that despite his uniform and his calling, he had retained some remnants of civilization. As my father did not survive Buchenwald, I do not know if he was ever told about us—but I do hope so, with all my heart.

On February 1, Schultz called all of us together—we were now 480, including eighty-two who could no longer get up from their sickbeds— and told us that we would be taken back to Stutthof. Since there were no trains available, however, we would have to walk a distance of 130 kilometers. In a reasonable manner he indicated that such a feat would not be possible for everyone and that the two physicians would therefore have to decide who could and who could not walk that far. He also added that he was told to bring back no more than about 250 of us.

Following his speech, he left the building. In the meantime, in small groups the women entered the physicians' large new examination room. When she saw the three of us come in, the Slovakian doctor did not waste words. She said that in view of my mother's recent illness and our general physical condition, she could not permit us to go along. Our pleas fell on deaf ears. She was adamant. At one point, Dr. Stein suggested timidly, "Perhaps just one of them?" "Absolutely not!" was the firm reply and with that she sent us out.

We were devastated. We knew what it meant to stay behind. We had come so far, and now this! Rumors ebbed back and forth; we saw some of the women smiling, others were crying, and during the next few days, when we no longer went to work, there was a constant stream of women going in and out of the doctors' office. Leah Granierer, who was my mother's age, told us that she, too, had been put on the "bad" list. However, she had gone back and had given the Slovak doctor a 20 rubel gold coin—not her own, but the last piece of value from beautiful, redheaded Mariasha Gershonowitz from Vilno, her son's girlfriend in Kaiserwald. Dr. Loewy pocketed the coin and put Leah Granierer on the "good" list.

Although we had nothing to buy our lives with, I decided to go back and appeal to the doctors once more, without mentioning what I knew about the gold coin. Nothing helped. Dr. Stein remained silent and Dr. Loewy said that we would be a burden to the other walkers, herself and Dr. Stein included, and "that's the way it is!" I realized then that there was no hope for us and that she meant to let us die. Yet, I could do nothing except curse her—a thing that I had never done before nor have I done since. In a mixture of Romany and Hungarian learned from the gypsies in Stutthof, I wished her the worst death possible! At least I had the satisfaction to see her face lose its smug expression. She turned white; being from Košice, she understood only too well what I had said. Dr. Stein was mystified, but I said nothing to her. I saw that she had no power to help us. Walking out, I knew that my mother, my sister, and I were doomed.

On February 9, the day before the departure of the "lucky" ones, the order was given that all those who were staying behind had to give up their shoes to those who would be leaving. We panicked even more if that was possible and so did others. I used the general confusion to play out my last card. First, I handed my good shoes to my mother who hid them insider her dress, which had gotten very big on her. Then, unnoticed by anyone, in stockinged feet, I ran upstairs to where the SS women spent their time. My luck held. Erika was on duty. She came out after I knocked and pointing at my feet, said "Are you crazy?" In my very best manner and holding back tears, I told her about the lists and the shoes and our wish to leave . . . after all, I could not tell her that I knew we were to be murdered; she was an SS woman and not to be trusted, even then. Still, I begged her, for the sake of both of our mothers, to save us! When she said, "I'll do what I can," the same wild hope surged through me as on the day I left Stutthof.

She handed me the key to a small room at the bottom of the stairs where cleaning utensils were kept and told me to get my mother and sister there. "Don't let anyone in until you hear my voice and don't give up your shoes just yet," she said, and I ran down and managed to get Mama and Rita to come to the little room. People were so busy with their own problems, the exchange of shoes, a few fights, and much unhappiness, that no one paid attention when we slipped out, one by one.

It could not have been more than an hour, although it seemed much longer, when Erika knocked and we opened the door. She smiled, and calling my mother "Mutti," told us to go back up and join the others. "There'll be an announcement in ten minutes," she said. "Don't worry about anything!"

We had hardly reached the teeming hall, when the *Kommandant*, accompanied by *Untersturmfuehrer* Roppert, the *"Standortarzt,"* that is, a physician, arrived. Schultz was smiling and Roppert addressed us gruffly, saying, "Everyone who believes he can walk all the way back to Stutthof, should be ready by next morning." Schultz added, "The women who are in the hospital will remain in Sophienwalde; they will be tended by two nurses."

It turned out that the nurses, the sisters Lucy and Edith Trampler from Vienna, had volunteered to stay behind. Also staying were two young girls from Kovno; the older one was in her ninth month of pregnancy, and her fifteen-year-old sister did not want to leave without her. Among the sick was Margit Reckler, who had been married in the ghetto to Percy Brandt, the famous Latvian violinist. This beautiful woman was only a shadow of her former self. Her equally beautiful daughter Eva could have walked, but she preferred to stay with her mother. Thus, a total of eighty-six women were left behind. Did we grieve for them? Did their fate upset us? I am sure we felt terribly sorry, but we were so caught up in making preparations for the journey, that we did not think of them. At least not just then.

People re-exchanged shoes, some cut up their blankets to make pants that would guard against the cold and did not have to be carried, the lucky ones baked potatoes, and there was a coming and going in the building; everyone was excited. Women such as us, who had faced certain death, were relieved and euphoric.

Three hundred ninety-four of us left on the morning of February 10, accompanied by the three SS women and fourteen guards. The two slim, blond Trampler sisters stood and waved to us, and they smiled.

They were dead only about three hours later. According to eyewitnesses interviewed by me in Dziemiany, all eighty-six had been put into two vans, and were taken to the forest at Lesno. A Latvian detachment had shot them there, leaving their bodies to be buried by the inhabitants of the village. Supervising the operation were *Sturmscharfuehrer* Schultz, our *Kommandant*, *Untersturmfuehrer* Roppert, the SS physician, and the *Unterscharfuehrer* of the guards, Nikolaus Knapp. Schultz and Knapp reached our straggling column on their bicycles several hours after we had left Sophienwalde.

While the *Unterscharfuehrer* behaved exactly as he had always done, screaming at us and at his men, it seemed that Schultz was no longer the same. He had aged in these few hours and never said a word to the marchers, nor did he joke, as was his custom. We were too busy putting one foot in front of the other to think much about this, nor could anyone among us believe that he had been party to murder. All we knew was that he had always been decent to us and had tried to alleviate our suffering.

After a short conversation with the three SS women, Schultz went on ahead, still on his bike, and arranged for a barn where we would spend the night.

We never got much rest. Unaccustomed to marching, many women had picked up snow from the side of the road to slake their thirst. Since there were no toilets, they now went behind the barn to relieve themselves and this went on all night. When morning came, a disgusted Schultz asked for ten volunteers to clean up the mess. He promised each a small jar of beet marmalade. My mother immediately volunteered. She needed the sweet stuff for Rita, who was clearly jaundiced. An old folk remedy for yellow jaundice is sugar, and Rita was not only yellow, but ran a fever as well. We tried to keep her sickness a secret and when several stragglers were permitted to ride on a wagon drawn by a horse, which Schultz had requisitioned from a farmer, my mother, distrustful and cautious, did not let my sister ride on it.

As we walked on that second day, I remember that some of the smarter women among us were puzzled by the direction we took. We were walking west, yet Stutthof was situated to the northeast of Sophienwalde.

While no one had been shot so far, even though Knapp was heard to say that he would shoot anyone who stopped walking, several women had not survived the first night and it did not look good for many others. Schultz ordered the two physicians to do their best, even though they, too, were affected by the march. As we stopped next to a barn where we would spend the second night, each of us received a slice of bread. We had walked only twenty-five kilometers in these two days, and already our strength was taxed to its limits. Again there were several deaths during the night. The bodies were left one on top of the other next to the barn.

We did not walk much on the third day. It was only February 12, but the day was unusually warm. The snow was melting and the ground under our feet turned into a morass. Since the majority of the women wore wooden clogs, they frequently fell. Whenever this happened, the *Unterscharfuehrer* prodded them with his rifle and made them get up and walk. He raved and ranted, but he did not shoot them. We believed that he must have had such orders from Schultz, who was still not quite his usual jolly self.

After we had walked ten kilometers that day, we arrived at the outskirts of Bütow, now Bytow, where Schultz found a very good, spacious barn for us and announced that we would rest there all of the next day. In addition, he sent Bertl Schwartz and her helpers to cook a potato soup for us at the nearby farmhouse.

Indescribably happy, Rita and I settled down. Our mother saw another large barn across the road and with her usual audacity went to investigate. Inside it was not a barn at all, but a barrack for American prisoners of war! Neither their guards nor our guards interfered when several other women followed my mother and went for a "visit." The Americans were shocked at the way we looked. Among them were two Jews from Brooklyn, New York. I was one of those who spoke a little English, and we told them some of what had happened to us in the last few years. They did not have much food either, but in a lovely gesture, they literally gave us the undershirts off their backs. I still have mine! Rita got a piece of soap with a swan on it.

The two doctors were quite busy the next day. Several women had died during the night; all of them had suffered from spotted typyhoid fever. Whenever the doctors looked at my mother, my sister, or at me, they averted their eyes. We never said a word to them and they never said a word to us. I could not forgive them, even though I was busy worrying about Rita. Although the beet marmalade, mixed with snow, had helped her, mother and I realized that it took all her willpower to march again on the next day of our journey.

Now we were marching north. After thirteen kilometers, the commandant ordered us into another barn. It was awful. It stank and it was filthy; when we found several corpses behind the barn, we realized that Jewish male prisoners had used it the night before. Schultz left to look for another barn but soon returned saying that he could not find anything.

When Resi Goldstein counted us the next morning, she at first believed that one woman had escaped. Her corpse, however, was soon found on top of the male corpses. The mystery of why she went outside to die in this way was never solved.

Weary in body and in spirit, we started marching once again. It snowed all day—big, wet flakes. At one point, while walking through a small town, several boys who had just come out of school, started pelting us with snowballs. Our obvious discomfort only increased their fervor. They called us vile names and their aim was quite good. Suddenly, out of the whirling snow an enormous *Schupo* (policeman) appeared and roared, "You miserable kids . . . stop it . . . stop it right now! Don't ever let me catch you again throwing snowballs at those unfortunate people . . . haven't they suffered enough?" The boys did stop and scattered, while he just stood there and looked at us, shaking his big head.

I remember the bitter tears I cried as I continued walking. His unexpected kindness and his recklessness in taking our part touched me to the core. I never cried when treated badly, but this show of sympathy for our plight made me fall apart.

After we had walked twelve kilometers, we were ordered to go into yet another barn. While it was better than the last one, there was very little straw and its roof and walls were dilapidated. In an attempt to make a joke, Rita said that she would be between Mama and myself and she would keep us warm since she still ran a high fever.

The next morning, February 16, we were each given a slice of freshly baked bread and Schultz looked very pleased with himself. This was a time when very few bakeries still operated and he seemed glad to have found one. Resi Goldstein came to us and gave Rita an additional piece of bread. We were stunned—it meant so much. As we stood lined up in front of the barn for the inevitable roll call, she said that eleven women had died during the night and that we numbered 365.

That day the weather was very good, the road was smooth, and we managed to walk thirteen kilometers. (The distances between the villages were clearly marked and I wrote everything down whenever we rested. My little stub of a pencil was my greatest treasure. I wanted to keep a record because I had promised my father that I would do so and because I wanted to read all this to him when the war would be over and when we would finally be together again. I never got that chance. But I did check the signs when I went back to that part of Poland and there were no mistakes. Only now, the signs have Polish instead of German place names.)

We continued walking, north by northeast. Our poor feet were like automatons. Step by step. Hoping not to fall behind and be prodded by a guard. Relieving ourselves at the edge of the road, oblivious to what anyone would think. Almost inhuman. But so were our conditions. Inhuman.

Another road, another barn, more dead. In between, it seemed that Schultz was in touch with Stutthof via telephone. A rumor had it that he talked about new orders to the women in front, and it must have been true for on Saturday, February 17, around noon, our march came to an end. After having walked eighty-three kilometers, we had arrived at the village of Gotentov, now Godętowo. There were 347 of us who had made it! Schultz told us that we were to stay here for a few days and that we would be joined by other prisoners, also on their way to the main camp.

Gotentov had a small camp, consisting of two parts. Half of the barracks were at the bottom of a hill next to a lake, and the other half were at the top of the hill. We could get water from the lake, but there was very little food for us. We received half a liter of soup each day; it was really only lukewarm, colored water. Every second day, we received a slice of bread.

After the arrival of other prisoners, the women who had come from Sophienwalde ended up in what was the worst barrack. It stood at right angles to the others and was very dilapidated. Before we came, all of the barracks had been home to forced laborers. They left only dirt behind; we found nothing that could be of use.

Among the arrivals over the next few days, we met the last remnants of Jews who had come from Riga to Stutthof on October 1, 1944. We could hardly recognize each other. The death toll in the coming weeks was very high. Conditions in Gotentov were the worst so far. People slept wherever they could find space, healthy and sick next to each other, some on bunks, some on the floor, and some on benches.

The barracks at the top of the hill housed the various SS personnel and all the commandants from the various camps who had walked. There was also a detachment of female German soldiers. They marched and sang while right below them we died *en masse* and grew weaker by the hour.

Our two physicians were given a room at the top as well. There were some other doctors who had been with the later arrivals and they, too, were quartered at the top. There was not much they could do for the many sick in the camp, since very little in the way of medication was available.

My sister had recovered from jaundice, but on March 6 I started to feel dizzy and passed out. Typhoid fever had caught up with me and the next three days are a blur. I was permitted to remain inside the barrack during roll call.

On Friday afternoon, March 9, Schultz came in while the others were

the women
him to get
and chil-
her that
ay me.
ched
ger
On

~ed me as "little roofer" and then said
~ well! You must pull yourself to-
~n the next few hours and you cannot
~der you to come along! You cannot stay

~st then, his speech seemed like a dream. I told
~d said, and it did not take long for orders to be
~d start marching once more. Mother went to look for
~ by now in her seventh month of pregnancy and quite
~rged her to make me walk, no matter what; she gave my
~arge piece of bread for the journey. I could not swallow solid
~ut I did drink the soup we were given and then, supported by
~nother and sister, I walked out of the camp.

Our two physicians stayed in Gotentov. We found out later that their room caught fire that same night, while they slept, and both of them perished in the flames. Of the other prisoners who stayed behind, only a handful were alive when the Russians came in late afternoon on the very next day. But contrary to what Schultz evidently believed, not one of them was killed.

I remember only snatches of this long, horrible night. I know that there were other prisoners, besides those from Sophienwalde. I remember seeing many soldiers, and hearing shots, both near and far away. Many times I begged my mother and sister to just let me lie down, to let go of me, to let me have peace, to let me die. They would not hear of it. Mother consoled me by saying that we would soon be allowed to rest, just like on our earlier march. Whenever someone fell behind, he or she was shot. Among the many other SS officers who accompanied this long, unwieldy column, Schultz was of no account, since his rank was comparatively low. He, Martha, Lotte, and bulky Erika walked at our side. "His" women were at the end of the column. According to my mother's estimate, there were no more than about 250 of us left.

Among the soldiers who passed us, walking toward what was evidently the frontline, were Austrians; their dialect made it obvious. My mother asked one of them for soup, and I heard her. For the rest of her life, she never forgot that I, delirious and surely at the end of my strength, said with all the arrogance I could muster, *"Mama, man bettelt nicht!"* (Mama, one does not beg!) She told the story many, many times and always added that the young Viennese soldier gave her a tin of soup for me, smiling as he did so, and obviously amused by what I had said.

There was the noise of fighting and it was not too far away. Schultz remarked to the women within hearing distance, "I am leading you to

freedom!'' My mother, unaware of his part in the murder o[...]
who had been left behind, or perhaps oblivious to it, advised[...]
out of his uniform; she promised to get him home to his wif[...]
dren. He thought about it for a while and then declined, telling[...]
he could not do so because, as he said, ''Someone is sure to be[...]
But I thank you!''

After having walked all night, about fifteen kilometers, we re[...]
the little town of Chinov, now Chynowie. An enormous barn, la[...]
than most others, next to a grassy slope, was to be ours for the day.[...]
that slope were many wagons, loaded high with household goods. The[...]
owners were trying to escape from the Russians. The barn contained[...]
several live horses, a few dead ones, and hundreds of dead and hunger-
crazed Jewish men and women, who had arrived a few days earlier.
Some of them were cutting pieces from the dead horses and were intent
on chewing the raw meat.

My mother put me into a fodder trough between two horses and told
my sister to stand right next to me so that I should not fall out. Meanwhile she stood at the barn's entrance, observant and alert. Suddenly,
in a changed voice, she said, *''Kinder, da kommen Russische Panzer!''*
(Children, Russian tanks are approaching!) Rita turned to me and said,
''Um Gottes Willen, die arme Mama hat den Verstand verloren!'' (For
God's sake, poor Mama has lost her mind!) But my mother was right
. . . the Russians had taken that obscure road, and freedom had come
for us.

Despite my weakened state and my illness, I wanted to savor this
long awaited moment. In my delirium, I found a truck full of sugar, but
eventually my mother coaxed me to come down. Then, together with
her and my sister and some other women, we stood on the square in
front of the barn and watched as the Russians brought out all the SS
men they could find in the houses behind the barn. Among us were
women who understood and spoke Russian and it was they who first
realized that the SS men would be shot at the edge of the road, where
the forest began, only a few meters from where we were standing.

When the Russians brought out Willie Schultz, pushing him to go
faster, it was one of ''his'' women, Mrs. Klara Schwab of Libau, who
tried to intercede for him. She, too, had no idea about what he had done
in Sophienwalde. The Russian officer in charge, to whom she spoke in
flawless Russian, accused her of being a German spy—she was a blond
woman and good looking even then—and he threatened to kill her, too,
if she continued to ask that Schultz's life be spared. She came over to
where we had gathered, and silently we stood by and watched as one

by one, the guards and the officers were shot, among them *Unterschar-fuehrer* Knapp and our commandant. Martha was nowhere to be seen, but Lotte and Erika were taken along on separate tanks.

The civilians of the town, as well as those who were on the slope, were ordered by the remaining Russians to put the dead SS men on a pile and then to do the same with the dead Jews who had expired in the barn. This was done. All those corpses, intermingled as they were . . . and there were no more differences. In death they were all equal.

For us, the living, freedom had come, with all its glories, with all its disappointments and the pain of finding out the extent of the Jewish people's destruction, with all its responsibilities, and with all of life's uncertainties.

There was one thing, however, we could be sure of: We would never, ever finish that road in Sophienwalde!

EDITOR'S NOTE

The foregoing vignette is a tribute to my mother, a lady of great courage. At the same time, according to Dena Abramovitz, senior librarian at YIVO (Yiddisher Institute For Wissenschaftliche Oyfgaben [Jewish Institute for Scientific Research]), it is a sorely needed account of what happened in Stutthof in that last year, when it became a "Jewish" camp. It is also an indictment of the so-called Latvian doctors, whose presence in Sophienwalde was such a shock to us. Furthermore, it presents a record of those many Hungarian women, who came from Auschwitz to Riga, then to Stutthof, and finally to that little village Sophienwalde . . .

In May 1989, at Kibbutz Shefayim, located between Haifa and Tel Aviv and founded by Latvian Jews, as I idly searched through their records, I came across a document dated May 30, 1945, of testimony given by one Margit Berger in Bukarest, Romania.

She describes how she was sent to Auschwitz in May of 1944, then to Riga, how she worked at a terrible camp in Poperwalen, then at a "Hungarian" camp in Dundaga, and how she finally came to Stutthof, Block 18. She testifies further that she was in Stutthof only about two weeks and was then taken to Sophienwalde, where she slept in a hut. She also describes the march to Gotentov, in February 1945, and finally, no doubt in answer to the official's question, she says that she was liberated together with Edith and Erszi Ordentlich from Cluj, Lenke Braun from Halmei, Roszi Kahan from Oreadea, and a Frau Hirschhorn with daughters Trudy and Rita from Vienna! She remembered our names, perhaps because a mother and two daughters were so unusual, and I was profoundly touched.

The vignette took a long time to write, necessitating several trips to Poland, where I visited Sophienwalde three times, went to Stutthof twice, and did some more research at the Historical Institute of Warsaw.

My own diary entries, written in 1944 and 1945, had seemed so complete at first, but as I continued in my research, I found that I and all the other women in our camp had known very little of what had been going on right under our noses.

I interviewed several Poles, some who had lived in the village at the time and some who were part of a Polish labor camp and had worked alongside us. My husband and I were guests of young Father Lehmann's parents. His aunt was there too and she told us that she had seen and had spoken to several of the poor Jewish girls who had slaved at building the road. I did not disclose to anyone that I, too, had been in Sophienwalde—all they knew was that I was doing research on the various camps in the vicinity and on the events of that time.

My husband Eric Schneider, born and bred in Kraków, Poland, was my able interpreter and both of us felt that there would be no point in disclosing my own painful story. It was only later, at the Stutthof archives, that we changed our minds. When the director of the archives, Magister Janina Grabowska-Chalka and her Assistant, Dr. Marek Orski, expressed reservations about some information that I said I had obtained, such as the march to Gotentov and the liberation at Chinov, I decided I had to tell them the truth.

Both Grabowska and Orski said they had read reports by witnesses, saying that all the women of Sophienwalde had been murdered in Lesno, in February 1945. When my husband told them that I was very much alive and that there were other survivors, they were stunned. Yet, I could see that they were still not sure. I asked for the records of August 9, 1944, the day of our arrival in Stutthof, and when these folios were brought up to Magister Grabowska's office, I pointed out the "SIPO–RIGA" *(Sicherheits Polizei-Riga)* entries for my mother, my sister, and myself, and many others who were well-known to me, some of them still alive, and others having perished during that last, terrible winter of 1944-45.

After that, there were no more doubts and I was given every document I asked for, including the many letters Schultz had written to Stutthof from Sophienwalde, always asking to be sent clothing for us, or towels, or even soap and medicine.

A reporter from Gdańsk, Miroslaw Piepka, wrote a long newspaper article about my return to Sophienwalde and Stutthof, with a picture of me. He entitled the story "Echoes of War."

A few months after my return to the United States, I received a letter from Father Lehmann, that first contact in my search for the secrets of Sophienwalde. He sent me his blessings, as well as his best wishes, and then he wrote, "My dear lady, I have seen your picture in the newspaper *Glos Wybrzeza*. I have read the account of your life, but I cannot understand how you could survive the hell of Sophienwalde. Please let me know!"

I hope he will read this story.

2

Arrest and Expulsion to Siberia

Baruch Minkowicz
(Translated from Hebrew by Isaac Leo Kram)

On June 12, 1941, when I went to work at the shoe factory Uzvara (it had previously belonged to Jacobson on Marias Iela) I saw a notice that the factory was to put all its trucks and drivers at the disposal of the regional Soviet Committee. Similar orders were given to many other enterprises in the city of Riga.

Somewhat worried, my mother and I went out around midnight. We noticed that the NKVD (Narodny Komissariat Vnutrennikh Del [People's Commissariat of Internal Affairs]) building on Brivibas Iela, which was usually lit up at night, was completely dark. Many trucks were parked on Brivibas at the corner of Gertrudas Iela, but all was dark. Yet, some trucks, two abreast, moved toward Krishian Baronu Iela. Apparently, these were the trucks that had been mobilized by the Party. Why were they here? What were they supposed to transport? To where?

A few hours later I was to find out.

Mother and I went home. We lived on Blaumanu Iela 3, in the building owned by Schiff and Mizroch. While standing at the entrance to our house, waiting for the night watchman to open it, we noticed similar activities on the corner of Blaumanu and Gertrudas Ielas. It was now one o'clock in the morning. We could see several civilians accompanied by a soldier leave the Party's building. This went on every five minutes

. . . four civilians and one soldier, easily recognized by his cap. The watchman seemed worried too.

We had gone to sleep and it seemed only a short time later that I was awakened by strong knocks at our door. There stood an armed soldier and four civilians who, after making sure that I was indeed Baruch Minkowicz, told me that they had an arrest warrant for me as an "undesirable element" and it was decreed that I was to be taken away from regions of the Soviet Latvian Republic. They said, "If your mother wishes to, she may accompany you. You have twenty minutes to pack your belongings. No more than one hundred kilograms." There was then a thorough search of my room, but I had long ago destroyed all Zionist literature, pictures from the life of our movement, and personal letters as well. They did not find anything incriminating. I asked permission to telephone my fiancée and tell her about my arrest, but my request was denied. Mother and I packed our belongings and it took us only thirty minutes, but then we had to wait several hours until the truck came to take us away. We were not allowed to speak to each other, and the men did not answer any questions either.

The truck came to our house at five o'clock in the morning. We took our valises and joined some other people already on the truck. Two fully armed Red Army soldiers were watching us, and the people on the truck looked rather scared. On our way across the Daugava River, we saw empty trucks coming back, evidently to pick up other people.

There was a huge traffic jam near the pontoon bridge. Our truck finally made it and continued on its way to the Tornkalns Railway Station. NKVD soldiers directed the trucks to the railway platforms. They were assisted by civilian Party members, some of whom were cruel, while others were more lenient. I was lucky. As our truck came to the platform, an old acquaintance of mine from high school and university days, and now a functionary, came over to me. He asked whether I was an "arrestee" or a "deportee." I told him that I had been arrested but that my mother was going with me. He then told me that we would be in separate cars and that I should repack our valises. To this day I am grateful to that man. If not for his advice, I would have taken both valises with me and my mother would have gone to Siberia without anything. Even before we descended from the truck, I repacked our valises, one for my mother and one for me, dividing our clothes.

Long lines of freight cars were on each side of the platforms. Each car had a tiny opening in the upper right corner and inside the car, on both sides of the entrance, mattresses were spread out. There was a hole in the floor, near the entrance, for the discharge of biological needs.

From all over Latvia, forty thousand people were taken away or left voluntarily in cars of that sort and among them were twelve thousand Jews!

My mother and I were separated; as she was taken to her car, I was pushed into another one that had already many people in it. As soon as it was filled, the door was shut and closed from the outside. I looked around and saw some of my acquaintances and even good friends. There was Samuel (Mulia) Markowitz, a medical student, the son of a noted physician.

In our car, there were also well-known Latvian personalities, such as the veteran State Controller Kaminsky, who was brought to the station straight from the hospital after a leg amputation; there was also the Latvian attorney Holtzmanis. He had become famous for his spirited defense of the "Bund" leader Rabinovitch, who was sentenced to death after the World War I for being a traitor. Holtzmanis won the case. Right now he was very excited and aggravated that he would be denied the fulfillment of his professional duties as lawyer for one of his clients, whose trial was set for the next day, June 14. (The severe conditions in the camps and his being torn away from his family hastened Holtzmanis's end. He died that same year. Having been one of the few Latvian prisoners for whom the Jews felt gratitude and even affection, his death was sincerely mourned.)

All day long the freight cars stood there and through the small opening we could see what was going on. Constantly new groups of prisoners and deportees were brought to the station and loaded onto the freight cars. The Tornkalns Station resembled a prison on wheels. There was, in addition, a stream of friends and relatives, who had surmounted all kinds of difficulties and came to say good-bye to their loved ones. The NKVD soldiers showed enough leniency to permit them to give clothing and food packages to those who would soon be leaving. They were permitted to speak to them as well, but only a few words. Most of these visitors were visibly shaken. "Mulia, the most important thing is that you should continue your studies at the university," exclaimed his mother who had come to see him one more time. Her pathetic words still ring in my ears for they were characteristic of our naiveté. We believed what the Soviet authorities said. . . . Upon transferring all those people, they indicated that there would be great freedom in choosing a vocation. Tragically, thousands like Mrs. Markowitz who were killed by the Germans and their Latvian collaborators, believed deep in their hearts that their lucky sons had been saved by the Soviets. They did not know that these young men expired far away in so-called labor

camps for the rehabilitation of prisoners because their tormented bodies
and souls succumbed to the rigors of camp life.

Thanks to the engineer's maneuvers to get us out of the station, we
were able to see the endless length of the train when we left during the
night. At dawn we reached Skirotava Station and we saw relatives and
friends standing on the platform. Their hearts must have told them that
this would be the last time to see their dear ones. The train moved
slowly. When we passed Krustpils, we saw trains similar to ours. It
became clear to us that we were witnessing a huge population transfer,
rather unusual for our region. Deep in Soviet Russia, this would not
have been a novelty, hence their amazing efficiency in carrying out such
an enormous task. In Daugavpils there was the same scenario: more
freight cars filled to capacity.

It did not take long to reach the old Latvian-Russian border. The
closer we came, the greater the depression. The suffering of the Latvians was almost palpable; they could not hide their tears when leaving
their fatherland. The Jews were downhearted too. All of us had left
someone behind, and all of us had been uprooted from our homes, losing most of our possessions in the process. We, the young Zionists,
were especially hurt for even with the open anti-Semitism in Latvia, we
had been able to lead a life of national consciousness, attend Hebrew
schools, join Zionist youth organizations, and prepare ourselves for
"*Alyah*" to Eretz Israel.

The very first thing we noticed in Russia, while peering out of the
little windows of the cars, was the abject poverty of the population. The
impression was one of desolation and shabbiness.

At the stations of Vitebsk and Smolensk, several trains passed us,
containing prisoners from Lithuania; among them were many Jews. We
concluded that they had met with the same fate.

After another three days, our train stopped at a small station called
Babino. As the doors of our car were opened, we saw that those cars
that contained our relatives who had decided to accompany the prisoners, including my own mother, were being attached to another train.
They left as we stood there, and none of us knew what their fate would
be.

We were surrounded by many guards. Among us were people of every
political affiliation. I saw many of Riga's Jews, wealthy businessmen
and industrialists sharing the fate of professionals, civic leaders, and
politically undesirables.

It was difficult to judge what the criteria had been that determined one's being arrested. At any rate, the percentage of Jews was out of proportion.

All the Zionist leaders were there, no matter whether right wing or left wing. I saw Zalman Rabinowitz, Dr. Reuven Hoff, Rudolf Kaplan, Jerachmiel Winnik, Zvi Garfunkel, engineer Abraham Ribowsky, and attorney Sali Levenberg.

The entire Betar Committee was there. One of the Betar members, the pharmacist Nahum Moskovski, had swallowed poison pills when the NKVD had come for him. He died in his own bed. How lucky he was! I also saw the Youth Bund leader Senia Braun, who was to die some time later in a labor camp. It seemed to me that many of the Latvian intelligentsia were here as well, including many political leaders, no matter whether from the right or the left. Now the members of the Ulmanis regime mingled with the progressives who had been out of power. Obviously, it made no difference to the NKVD. They had taken all the undesirable elements and had left behind the trustworthy citizens. Alas, just a few weeks later, these so-called trustworthy persons stood in their windows and shot the retreating Soviet soldiers in the back; after that, they collaborated with the Germans in the persecution and extermination of the Jews of Latvia.

Under heavy guard, we started walking. The local peasants stared at us in amazement . . . they must have been astonished by our elegant clothing. All day long we walked under the hot sun, plagued by thirst. We reached camp Yuchnovo late at night. It was huge, had large barracks surrounded by barbed wire fences, with a manned watchtower in each corner. By dawn our guards had turned us over to the camp authorities; we were identified, our belongings were registered, especially monies and valuables, which were to be returned after the sentences were served. Some were indeed . . . if the prisoner was still alive . . .

The barracks were not very clean. There were long lines of two-tier bunks with mattresses, but the passages between the bunks were almost too narrow for two people to pass each other. We slumped down on our assigned bunks and fell asleep. For most of us it was to be the last real sleep we were to get, since the camp was infested with lice. We were soon infested as well and those tiny creatures did not let us rest for long.

We were fed three times a day and did not go hungry. What we were hungry for was news from home, but we had neither newspapers nor radios. It seems to me that around June 22 several strong men from each barrack were ordered to fill up sacks with sand, which were to be placed on the roofs of the barracks. We also had to fill up barrels with water and we sensed that something had happened, or that war was imminent.

The camp had a separate section, partitioned off with high wooden boards, which held former officers of the Latvian and Estonian armies. On the day we filled those bags with sand, we saw them being taken out of the camp.

By the middle of July, all of us were ordered to assemble in the courtyard. In a hurried fashion we were marched back to the railroad station, put on freight cars together with our belongings and, facing east, we were off again. As we passed a village not too far from Babino, we saw signs on the houses, saying, "We will fight the enemy on his own soil" . . . "We do not want strange lands but we will not give up our own" . . . "Death to the German invaders." . . . Now we knew. There were no more doubts . . . There was no more friendship between Hitler and Stalin . . . The war had begun. Yet, we were puzzled. Why did they rush us out of our camp? After all, we were in the region of Tula or Kaluga, which was far away from the border. Was the Red Army retreating?

The car was cramped, the heat was unbearable, and the food was bad. We were given salty herrings but only very little water. I remember that Zvi Garfunkel suffered so badly that we started fearing for his life. The nights were somewhat better.

After only two days, our train stopped at an outlying freight station of Moscow. It was lit up, even though the city was being attacked from the air; we could hear the sounds. The Latvians with us did not hide their glee, but for us Jews there was no reason to be happy. In the morning, we were on the move once more, and now the questions that had been on our minds all along, started to surface. Where were our relatives who accompanied us to Russia? Where were we being taken?

Our condition worsened; the food as well as the water portions got even smaller, and the heat rose. We were getting weaker and thought that this might be our end. Alas, this was only the beginning.

The first victim was Segal, who had lived on Brivibas Iela. He had been taken from his home while recovering from a serious stomach operation and his suffering on the train, especially when he had to perform his biological functions, was indescribable. The physicians among us pleaded with the guards that he be taken to a hospital, but they turned a deaf ear and Segal died somewhere between Moscow and Molotov-Perm.

Other trains passed us, also heading east. We saw that they were occupied by women and children. They had their luggage and it turned out that they were refugees from Latvia and Lithuania. They, however, were the relatives of Soviet civil servants and military men and were now being evacuated from the danger zones. But there were also other trains somewhat like ours, and sometimes we were able to exchange a few words with the passengers. In this way, I found Nathan Michlin, who told me that he had gone into hiding after my arrest; he was found within a week. It turned out that many people on his train were known to me, since most of them were Zionists. They came from Libau, (Liepaja), Windau (Ventspils), and Latgale. I never saw Nathan Michlin again, but a long time after my own release, I learned that he had been taken to the Vyatka camps in the Kirov region, where he died in 1942 of starvation and exhaustion. He was a veteran Betar leader and at one time a member of Betar's International Central Committee. An entire generation of Betar members was inspired by his burning love for Eretz Israel and his boundless devotion to the Jewish people.

A few days later the train arrived at the Solikamsk railroad station, the last point of our current journey. Solikamsk was a medium sized city, northeast of Molotov-Perm, and connected to it by a separate railroad. Solikamsk was known for its salt mines, but for the Jews of Latvia and Lithuania, it assumed another, sinister fame, for here thousands of people died of physical and spiritual tortures. The same was true of the Vyatka camps. We were witnessing how people could be killed without firing a shot, and our tormentors were quite successful in this liquidation process. Two thirds of our people were buried there and in Vyatka, and the dying started in the winter of 1941–42.

The first prisoners we encountered in the four camps that made up the Solikamsk complex were Polish Jews who were exiled here in 1939 when the Russians occupied the eastern region of Poland. Their pathetic appearance, their accounts of camp life, and the hard labor that had taken its toll on them did not give us much to hope for.

Before we were separated into four groups, the well-known Riga attorney Rosofsky died. He was the first of many to be buried in far off Solikamsk.

After the separation into groups, we were marched to the four camps, often never to see each other again. Our group marched for twenty-four hours before we reached our destination. We were totally exhausted. The camp was enclosed by barbed wire and contained several wooden barracks. Here, too, there were manned lookout towers. Swampland was all around us. The name of the camp was Chertyoz. It was situated in a valley and the humidity increased as we got nearer; so did the swarms of mosquitoes.

After registration and a search, we were permitted to enter the barracks, which were set up similar to those at Yuchnovo, except that they were darker and dirtier. Here, too, lice reigned supreme. For this reason, many of us slept on the ground outside, but this led to sicknesses. For those who contacted pneumonia, it was tantamount to a death sentence. The lack of proper medication prevented our physicians from giving first aid, let alone treatment for pneumonia. The next two people to die were the banker Levstein and Zalman Rabinowitz, who had been one of the leaders of the general Zionists in Latvia and also the director of the stock company Rapid. It was very depressing, for Rabinowitz was not only highly esteemed in Riga, but even here, in the camp, everyone looked to him for advice.

Taking advantage of the fact that our guards were busy elsewhere, we tried to have a proper funeral for him, Levstein, and some others. The prisoners assembled along the barbed wire fence and I offered a brief eulogy for Rabinowitz. The well-known owner of a Riga Bakery, Tuvia Baran, led us in saying Kaddish. We thus observed the rules of our tradition.

After that funeral, however, the camp authorities forbade us to give this last honor to our departed comrades. In addition, death itself became commonplace.

The daily routine in camp seldom varied. At first, we were kept inside to do the usual camp chores, such as sawing wood for the kitchen and bathhouse, landscaping the grounds, drawing water from the wells, and raking the soil between the fences; in this way, the footprints of escapees would be visible. Since the work was not hard, we did not feel the lack of proper food. We were given 400 grams of bread a day, coffee in the morning, and soup both at lunch and at supper. Unfortunately, these optimum conditions were only temporary, for we were told that most of us would be sent to work outside the camp.

Around this time there occurred an event that upset us greatly. As we were counted three times a day, it became immediately apparent one day that a prisoner was missing. It was Meyerson-Simone, the author of *The Last Generation of Enslavement*. He had been a seller and buyer of used books in Riga, was highly educated and knowledgeable, but somewhat weird. The idea of escaping had been in his mind for some time, but he lacked a definite plan. He never had an answer to our realistic questions, such as, "Where will you go to?" or "Where will you hide?'' or ''What will you do after you escape?'' Many of us had implored him to give up these plans, since they were doomed to failure. Yet, despite all this, he had taken the risk. The camp was quite busy for a few hours, we saw all the functionaries, there was triple the amount of soldiers, and last, but not least, there were the German shepherd dogs. He was soon caught, prosecuted, and since his crime carried the death penalty, we never saw him again.

By the beginning of September, all able-bodied prisoners were transferred to camp Prizim (pressure) and it lived up to its name. We were separated into groups, some to labor in the forest and others to work at constructing an electric power station. The work was very hard, the days were very long, but there was only little food and it was bad. The weather was not too good either, for the mornings were already freezing, but at noon we were scorched by the sun. We were warned by long-time prisoners to watch our health. One ten-year veteran told us that only 40 percent would be able to survive the first few months. His words assumed great importance when the real cold weather arrived and our bodies required more calories than we were given. In addition, the cold also brought more sicknesses, such as edema in our feet, ulcerating sores on our bodies, and various other ills, unknown to us until then. Yet, the authorities demanded that we fulfill our work quotas, while our doctors felt compelled to let us stay in camp, since it was obvious that we could hardly walk at times.

We became depressed as we realized that no one cared for us, or for the high mortality rate of the camp. People asked themselves, ''Will my strength endure?'' and knew that only their stamina would carry them through. I, too, became ill and was exempted from slave labor for a few weeks; this undoubtedly saved my life.

Others were not so lucky and I feel it is my duty to mention their names, at least as far as I can remember. Sali Levenberg died from a serious case of furunculosis. He had been very active with the Hakoah Sports Club. He was good natured and trustworthy and always ready to share whatever he had with his friends. Mulia Markowitz died on April 20, 1942. He had been in the same car with me on that first day. His arrest was due to his having been the last head of the Hasmoneah Student Association. In camp he worked as a medic at first but was later sent to do hard labor. Very soon he became totally disabled. When he was finally exempted from work, it was too late. He moved with great difficulty and dragged himself around the camp, emaciated and hungry. On April 19 the camp's commandant noticed him and said sternly, ''Enough already, Markowitz! You are only pretending to be ill. To-

morrow you go back to work in the forest!'' Despite his pains, Mulia
was chased out of the barrack, and after only a few steps, collapsed. At
first they let him lay there, but when it became apparent that he was
unconscious, he was carried back in. The camp doctor's ministrations
were to no avail and thus the former medical student who had "feigned"
illness, died without regaining consciousness.

Much later, when my status was changed from prisoner to deportee,
I found out about the death of Rudolf Kaplan, who had been a well-
known personality in Latvian Zionist circles. While he did not join any
of the organizations, he contributed generously to all of them. He never
turned down an appeal for funds. In fact, due to his initiative and support, the boat *Theodore Herzl* was acquired—the first Jewish boat in the
Baltic Sea. A number of Betar members from Latvia and Estonia received their seafarers' training on it, and later some of them served on
Israel's merchant marine boats and also warships.

By the end of 1942, after he had been freed already, and now lived
as a deportee, Zvi Garfunkel died. He was known to everyone in Riga,
for he had been the principal of the Hebrew Grammar School for many
years. He was a highly regarded pedagogue and a friend of Jewish youth.
Whenever there was infighting between the different groups, it was Garfunkel who made peace. I myself attended lectures by him on Hebrew
literature. After the war, his surviving students in Israel said the Kaddish for him.

In February and March of 1942, seven months after the arrests in
Riga, the judicial inquiries began. It was only now that many among us
found out why we had been arrested and were persecuted by the Soviet
government. It turned out that almost all of us were being tried for
"crimes" committed before the Red Army had even entered Latvia in
1940! It was enough to have been a member of the Jewish Club in Riga,
or belong to the sports clubs Maccabi or Hakoah or the tennis club
Ritak. Some were condemned for having studied in foreign universities,
or belonging to Zionist Chalutz organizations from 1924 to 1929. Former store owners were considered counterrevolutionaries, enemies of
the working class, or bourgeois. Even worse off were rich industrialists,
and Social Democrats. They were branded as enemies of the Russian
people. When they complained about the camp conditions, which ran
counter to Russian judicial codes, they were told that the laws were
written for the working class and not for them!

In March my own case came up too. The accusations were that (1) I
was a member of an anti-Soviet youth organization, (2) I had participated in educating Jewish youth in the spirit of Zionism, whose goals

were to serve international bourgeoisie and British imperialism, and (3) since Zionist organizations continued their work underground during the 1940–41 Soviet reign, I had concealed my knowledge of the Betar organization's doings. They thus tried to show that I had been part and parcel of counterrevolutionary activities.

For five grueling hours the prosecutor tried to get me to admit to these "proven" charges. I, on the other hand, categorically denied that I had done anything illegal. I did say that I had been involved in Zionist activities prior to the Soviet reign in Latvia, and I insisted that the establishment of a Jewish State would replace the British mandate. I even quoted Stalin, but it was to no avail. The prosecutor kept insisting that striving to create a Jewish State was indeed a counterrevolutionary activity. I therefore refused to sign the protocol, but instead signed a statement containing my own words. I was then told that I would hear from them in due time.

By the end of April 1942, we were transferred from Camp Prizim back to the Chertyoz camp. The invalids were placed on horse-drawn carts, but the rest of us had to walk. Since the snow had started to melt by then, we were often up to our hips in ice cold water, which resulted in many deaths from pneumonia and exhaustion. I remember the death of engineer Kalgut, who was my foreman. Later on, his son perished in a tragic accident. While working in a far northern corner of the Krasnoyarsk Province, he was engulfed by an enormous snowstorm called *Purga*. It carried him away and he was never found.

We met many friends in Chertyoz whom we had not seen for eight months, but we hardly recognized each other. We had changed so much! We talked about those who were no longer alive, among them the attorney Philip Latzky, Max Taubin, engineer Yitzchok Taubin, who had been the chairman of the Riga Technikum alumni, and Jerachmiel Winnik, one of the leaders of the Zionist Socialists in Riga. As early as December 1941, Winnik had been called to the prosecutor in Solikamsk. They did not have to sentence him . . . he died just a short while later.

Then, in August 1942, I was called back to Solikamsk and was given the verdict: As a socially dangerous element according to paragraph 58.4 of the Soviet Penal Code, I was sentenced to five years exile in the Siberian province of Krasnoyarsk.

Others, like myself, also received their sentences during the summer, and so, by the end of August, together with one hundred other men, I set out on the road to my place of exile. Other groups had already left; they went to either Kumi or Krasnoyarsk. The trip from Solikamsk to the various places of exile was another nightmare. This time we traveled in *Stolipin* railroad cars, a residue of the prison cars from the days of the Czars. They were regular railroad cars divided into compartments that were separated by metal grids, and fourteen to sixteen persons were squeezed into each compartment, which could normally only hold eight. The windows were closed and we almost suffocated. Twice a day, we were allowed to get out of the compartment and attend to biological needs. Complaints and pleas were totally ignored. We did not even feel hunger pangs, but the thirst was terrible.

After several days in the *Stolipin* cars, we arrived at the prison of Sverdlovsk. First a bathhouse, then prison cells. . . . we felt like we were in paradise, even though we had to sleep on the floor. We were permitted to go for a walk in the courtyard, the food was not too bad, but the one thing that depressed us was the fact that the prison authorities cared far more for the real criminals than for us, the Zionists or Social Democrats.

A few days later, we were off again; this time we were taken to the railroad station in prison vans called "black crows." Once again we boarded the *Stolipin* cars and after a tortuous ride, we reached Novosibirsk.

All I remember is getting to the station and from there to a transit prison. To my amazement, I woke up in a clean room with many beds and many strange people. A young physician, himself a prisoner, explained what had happened to me. No sooner had I entered the bathhouse when I fainted. They could not revive me and so, since I seemed to be very ill, I was transferred to the prison hospital. A second man of our group, also ill, was in the adjacent room. He was the elderly Altermann, former owner of the factory "Boston" in Riga. During all these months of imprisonment, his stamina and endurance never ceased to amaze me. He did the hardest jobs and never got sick. Yet, the rigors of being moved around in such a fashion were too much for him. He died in that prison hospital; his hopes and dreams to see his family again were never realized.

I was in the prison hospital for over two weeks and so missed the departure of my group. With another group, I boarded the *Stolipin* cars once more. After traveling for twenty-four hours, we reached Krasnoyarsk. It was early morning but we were expected. The chief officer of the NKVD told us that we would be sent to different sections of the region, across the Yenisei River. He would see us there in about ten days, in order to hand us our official documents. Although we were still deportees and subject to government supervision, we were no longer prisoners, a fact that was borne out by the absence of guards. We felt better.

At the transit point, we were pleased to find some of the people who had come here before we did and while we did not find our immediate families, many of us found out where they were. For the most part, they, too, were living in the region of Krasnoyarsk, District of Novosibirsk, in the town of Narim. We heard that the majority of them were in good health, even though they had gone through very difficult times. We were also told that some Latvian Jews had managed to flee only hours before the Nazis took over Latvia; they were in Central Asia. We also heard a rumor that a committee had been founded in Palestine to assist Latvian Jews, including refugees and deportees. Upon hearing news like this, our hearts were filled with hope and we started to believe in our future. In the meantime though, our lives were still far from comfortable, for even if we had our piece of bread and a few potatoes, we were not considered citizens with equal rights and we did not yet know that entire families of deportees and refugees had been destroyed.

One such family was that of Alter Abramowitz. His wife Mina was the sister of the famous gynecologist Dr. B. Hertzfelt. Alter was sent to Solikamsk, his wife and their younger son ended up in Narim. Their older son Isaak, however, was not at home when the family was taken away and thus avoided arrest. When the Germans attacked, Isaak voluntarily joined the Latvian Division of the Red Army and died as a hero in battle. After fifteen months at camp Solikamsk, the father was sent into exile at Kumi. He managed to establish contact with his wife and younger son in Narim but died shortly afterward. A short time later, Mina fell sick with pneumonia and died too, leaving the boy orphaned. All alone and with no one to care for him, the boy succumbed to tuberculosis. Thus, an entire Jewish family was destroyed, just because the head of that family had been a landlord in Riga!

Another tragic death was that of Professor Paul Mintz who had been State Comptroller of Latvia in the early years of independence and later professor of law at Riga University, a post he kept even during the Soviet reign. He and his family were exiled to Siberia, to the city of Kansk in the Krasnoyarsk Region. A year later he was arrested by the NKVD and imprisoned in the labor camp of Reshoti, where he died soon thereafter.

All of us were waiting anxiously for the end of the war. When our hopes were finally realized, the remnant of Latvian Jewry, still alive in Russia, started to trickle back. They learned what had happened to those who had been left behind and found only a few surviving Jews in Riga in 1946. It was almost too much to bear: At the time when the remaining Jews in Latvia were being murdered by the Germans and their devoted Latvian collaborators, another part of Latvian Jewry perished in the Soviet Union from hard work, cold, hunger, and untreated epidemics. They died in the regions of Solikamsk, the camps of Kirov and Vyatka, and they died in the regions of Krasnoyarsk, Novosibirsk, Tomsk, and the far north.

Tragically, very little was left of that vibrant Jewish community of Latvia; gone were relatives, neighbors, and friends.

They live only in our memory.

EDITOR'S NOTE

Baruch Minkowicz was one of the lucky ones, for in 1943 he was reunited with his mother as well as with his fiancée, Frieda Finkelmann. They got married very soon thereafter, and their son Eliahu was born in Siberia in 1945.

Two years later, without ever having gone back to Riga, the family was permitted to leave for Poland, since Dr. Minkowicz's father, who had come to Leningrad from Pinsk in 1920, had always retained his Polish citizenship.

They spent the next three years in Otwock, near Warsaw, where Baruch and Frieda both worked at a Jewish children's home. Their mission was to find Jewish children who had been given to Christians for safekeeping and whose parents had subsequently been murdered by the Germans. Dr. Minkowicz told me in October 1990, in Israel, that this work of "repatriating" Jewish children to Israel represented his "finest hour."

In 1950, the family moved again, but this time they left inhospitable Poland for the State of Israel. Another son, Nathan, was born there in 1952. Dr. Minkowicz and his two sons, lawyers like their distinguished father, are partners in a prestigious law office.

The old Mrs. Minkowicz died in Tel Aviv, in 1962. She considered herself a lucky woman.

The foregoing story of their arrest and expulsion appeared in 1953 in a longer version in *Yahadut Latvia*, published in Israel by the Association of Latvian and Estonian Jews.

3

Julia's Story

Julia Robinson

The war between Germany and Russia began on June 22, 1941. On June 23, my parents had a chance to escape from Riga. On that night, my father was called to the chief of the Soviet Military Project of the National Defense Committee, where he worked as a driver for the supply department. (In 1940, when the Soviets occupied Latvia, father had to find a job, since his family's business, like so many others, was nationalized. Due to his fluency in Russian, German, and Latvian, and because he knew his way around the city very well, he was hired to be the driver for the supply department.)

When father arrived at the chief's office, he found it in chaos, with everyone preparing to evacuate. Families had been brought to the building and were taken by vans to Riga's train station. "Take my car and bring your wife here," the chief told my father. "She can join the wives of the military personnel, while you will drive me to the Russian border. But you have only half an hour before we depart."

Father drove to his apartment through the streets of the darkened city at breakneck speed. Bombs were exploding and shots rang out. The *Aisargis*—Latvian pro-Nazi nationalist army members—were shooting from the rooftops at the departing Soviets.

Father and mother had lived with his parents since their marriage. That evening my mother's mother was there too, but her father was out of town. He had gone to Mitau (Jelgava), but the roads to Riga were closed and so he could not come back.

When father came in, the family was in the darkened kitchen, anxiously waiting for news. He told them about the impending departure of the Russians and of his chief's offer. Although he was able to convince my mother to come with him, no amount of begging helped with his parents or his mother-in-law. They refused to leave Riga. In fact, his father felt that there was nothing to fear and that their Latvian friends would take care of them. While they had heard stories, they did not believe what people from occupied Poland had related. At the time it was hard to imagine that the Germans really meant to murder all the Jews.

The last thing my mother remembered was how her mother ran after her and on the stairwell said, "Hennelle, take some chocolate for the road. You might get hungry."

Needless to say, all four of my grandparents, as well as an uncle and most of my relatives on both sides of the family were shot or burned alive by the Germans and their Latvian collaborators during the first few months of the war.

For the next three years my parents were refugees in Russia, wandering from town to town at first until they joined father's sister Rosa and her family in Frunze, Kirghiz SSR. They, too, had managed to escape. While her husband was drafted and was fighting at the front, Rosa was living at a collective farm near Frunze with her two children and her cousin Ania and family.

In March 1943 my father was drafted too. When he left, my mother was pregnant. I was born in Frunze on January 12, 1944. My cradle was a suitcase standing in a room inhabited by seven people.

Within the first weeks of my birth I contracted pneumonia in both lungs. Medicine was hardly available. Because of the general starvation, mother had little milk to feed me, and to get some at the local market was almost impossible. She did not have any money either.

I was totally dehydrated and I was dying.

The physician in charge of the children's hospital felt sorry for my mother and, contrary to rules, let her stay with me.

For almost half a year, my mother sat by my crib, watching over me. I was kept alive by blood transfusions given to me from her to the veins on my head. During the day she covered me with gauze to protect me from the "evil eye" of other women whose babies had died. Some of these unfortunates would stop by my crib and check with mother to see if I was still alive.

Everywhere around us were hunger, lice, and death.

One day, a man who looked like a vagrant showed up at the hospital. His body was a bag of bones, covered with filthy rags. His reddish beard and dirty hair were full of lice, his skin was covered with sores, and his eyeglasses hung on handmade wires.

This man was my father! He had just been released from a Siberian coal mining camp, where he had been sent after the army discharged him because of his poor eyesight.

When a commission checked on the inhuman conditions at the camp, father decided to ask them to permit him to fight despite his weak eyes. Anything was better than the camp! Standing in line and waiting to speak to the committee, he noticed an old upright piano in a corner of the room. He went over to it with great excitement and began to play. Four years had passed since he had touched a piano, but he was still good at it and even though several keys were missing, it sounded wonderful.

At first he played classical music. Then, as he switched to popular tunes and Russian folksongs, everyone in the room moved closer and listened to the nostalgic melodies.

One member of the commission, a female physician, made her way through the crowd. She asked my father who he was, where he came from, and why he was in a place like this. He explained that he was a refugee from Riga, Latvia, and that he used to play the piano before the war. He also told her that the army had dismissed him when they found out that his eyesight was so poor. The doctor took my father into the examination room, where she demonstrated to the other members of the commission how the conditions in the camp had seriously damaged a human being. The fact that he was considered an artist helped to get him released and as soon as he received the official discharge papers, he asked to be sent back to Frunze, where almost a year earlier he had left his pregnant wife.

His wish was granted. They gave him travel papers, two slices of bread, a thin slice of pork, and with that he set out on his way back to Frunze to look for my mother. It took him three days and nights to travel through the endless Siberian flatland, almost freezing to death for lack of warm clothing. Once he reached Frunze, he found out that mother and I were at the hospital and there, by the hospital window, my parents were reunited again. It was April 1944.

Neither of them said a word. My mother picked me up and on outstretched hands she showed her husband his little baby girl. They looked at each other, hardly believing that they were both alive, full of pain and grief for what they had suffered and what they had lost. Their eyes searched each other for any trace of the people they used to be once upon a time.

My mother, Henny Shrage, came from a family of a strong Germanic background, the Kurlaenders. Before the war, she and her family lived in Mitau, a small town about one hour's train ride from Riga.

The Shrages kept a strong Jewish tradition, although only German and Latvian was spoken in their home. The matriarch of the family was my great-grandmother Havah-Leah Shrage, called Lina. Widowed at age twenty-five, she never remarried but took charge of the family business, built stores and houses in Mitau, and ran a matzot bakery that supplied matzot to all of Kurland. Lina was a strong and beautiful woman and very few people dared to contradict her. One of her sons was my grandfather Nehamje Isser Shrage. He was a shrewd business man. He owned a store in Mitau and some real estate, and he was a talented tailor as well. His mother had insisted on each of her children having a skill. Nehamje was on very friendly terms with the local Germans, but in the thirties, with the spread of Nazi propaganda, they broke off all contact with Jews, no matter how close and strong their relations had been. In fact, many Latvians in that part of the country considered themselves German and went back to Germany in 1939.

Nehamje Isser's wife, my grandmother Sarah Mary, was a graduate of the Czarist gymnasium, a rare thing for a Jewish girl in those days. They had three children: my mother and two boys. The younger boy was born an invalid and was kept at home with a nurse until the war started. He was shot at the hospital with other crippled children. The other boy, Shimon, was only fourteen when he and his father Nehamje Isser were burned alive in the local theater in Mitau in the fall of 1941.

The fate of my grandmother was different. When my mother met her governess Zelma in Riga, upon her return in 1945, she was told that grandmother had lived in the ghetto, sharing a room with a family blessed with eight children. Zelma gave her food and she shared it with the children. She was killed in November 1941, during the first big *Aktion*.

My father's name was Aron Gindin. His family came to Riga from Siberia in 1920. Originally they had lived in Bielo Russia, but the pogroms there had driven them to Siberia. My father had two older sisters, Rosa and Sonia, and two younger brothers, Ruben and Michael. Ruben was drafted into the Latvian army in 1940 and was shot by the Latvian nationalists in June 1941 when the war started. Michael survived and now lives in Israel.

Father's family owned a large tailor shop in Riga. Shortly before the

Russians took over, they opened a clothing store as well. Father was a self-taught musician and hoped to become a concert pianist. The war interrupted these plans.

After their miraculous reunion in Frunze, my parents waited for the day when they could go home. In October 1944, the Soviet army liberated Riga, and in January 1945 my parents returned to Riga. Although the war was over as far as the territories of the Soviet Union were concerned, the same could not be said for my parents. Even their own city was no longer the place they had known before the war. Most of their families had been murdered and their property, amassed over many years and generations, was lost forever.

They could have left. In fact, they had a chance to escape to the West through Poland, with false passports, but my mother vetoed the idea since I was barely one year old, and she was afraid that I would cry and thus endanger the people who tried to cross the border. And so we stayed behind until all avenues to the West were closed. There was nothing else to do except pick up the pieces and start life all over again.

My mother did not have a profession. All my father knew was music, and even that not in any formal way. He now had to feed a family, and at first he did all kinds of jobs.

During the day he worked for a government agency that helped survivors locate their possessions. At night, in order to earn some more money, he played piano at a fashionable restaurant. As we had no place of our own, we had to stay with friends, sleeping on the floor.

Through the agency where father worked, he managed to prove that the apartment on Elizabetas Iela, today's Kirova Iela, had belonged to his parents. It was now occupied by a judge and his wife. They had received it from the Germans and refused to leave when asked to do so. One day, father called on the superintendent of the building and asked to be taken up to the apartment. He rang the doorbell and announced that he was from the police. When the judge opened the door, father wedged his foot in, thus preventing the man from closing it in his face. With the superintendent as his witness, father showed the judge the official papers proving that this apartment belonged to him once again. Meanwhile mother was waiting downstairs, with me in her arms. The judge and his wife had to pack up and leave.

We moved in immediately, although all the rooms were empty. My grandparents' furniture and clothes were all gone. Suddenly more open, the superintendent told my father that when the Nazis had moved in, they forced my grandmother to become their maid and serve them. Both she and my grandfather were later murdered at Rumbuli.

When he found that the superintendent knew so much, father asked him some very probing questions. Eventually, the man "found" some of grandfather's suits and my grandmother's fur coat among his own things. He claimed that the remainder of my grandparents' possessions were taken by the Nazis.

This apartment was the very place where my parents had gotten married in 1940 and where they had said such a hurried good-bye to their loved ones. We lived there from 1945 to 1946, and it was the only time in my life when I had my true family—my real father and my mother—under one roof.

Only one year later, my mother met another man, also a survivor, and they fell in love. My father gave her the desired divorce and she married Boris Rabiner, who became my stepfather and who actually raised me. Mother and I moved into his apartment on Brivibas Iela, at the corner of Latshplesha.

Despite the divorce, my parents remained on friendly terms and my father and I spent every weekend together. He was an interesting looking man, always dressed fashionably, and loved to entertain. He introduced me to a Bohemian life, to the world of music, opera, and the theater.

My stepfather Boris was a much more practical man. He had lost his mother when he was only six, and his father and three sisters were killed by the Germans. Witnesses told him that the members of his family were seen walking to their death holding each others' hands. The only members left of my stepfather's family were his brother Abrasha, whom he found in 1947, and his cousins Zalman and Sterna Rabiner.

I never had a problem of loyalty between my two fathers. I called them both "Papa" and was never uncomfortable to show my affection for one in front of the other.

My beautiful mother was a very pedantic woman. Order in the house and cleanliness were her obsessions. If anything was misplaced or moved, she would notice and make a fuss. She was a very giving person and a wonderful friend to many. She had tremendous insight into everything that concerned us.

My earliest childhood memories go back to the summer of 1947. We rented a place on the beach, in Dzintary. One day I was playing with other children in the sand when suddenly a woman began to shout, "the Nazis are coming." Everyone started to run and I was left alone. I could see a group of men approaching me and I, too, started screaming. It turned out that they were construction workers, and the woman had mistaken them for prisoners of war who had done this work, wearing similar clothes. This image and the fright has remained with me to this day.

Until 1947 we lived quite well by Soviet standards. My stepfather had a very responsible position manufacturing paper, a skill he had learned in his father's factory while still a youngster. He made a lot of money.

Our apartment on Brivibas was a communal one in which we occupied two rooms. One was our bedroom, where the three of us slept and the other was the living room. In the middle of it stood a porcelain stove called *burzuika,* which kept us warm during the winter months. The third room belonged to our neighbors.

Mother could afford to have a governess for me. Her name was Bluma Kocherginsky and she had been in Siberia during the war, where she lost her little girl. She came back to Riga with her little boy and made ends meet by looking after other people's children. She loved to take me on long walks and tell me about Jewish life in Riga before the war.

By the end of 1947, a catastrophe befell us and many others. Both of my fathers were arrested at the same time. It was the famous Golin case. More than fifty people were arrested and it was soon clear that it was a show trial, directed against Jews. My stepfather was accused of commercial dealings and my father was accused of keeping money for a friend. For these "crimes," father was sentenced to two years in prison and my stepfather to an incredible five years.

My mother was in her third month of pregnancy. We had absolutely no support and as the ruble was just then devalued, even our savings meant very little. Bluma stayed with us for a while without pay; then she went back to Siberia to join her husband.

After mother gave birth to a boy, she took a job of painting colored borders on batik handkerchiefs. She had to blow oil paint through a glass tube all day, and very often she brought her work home to make a few extra rubles for us. I watched her work, but the stench of the oil paint was unbearable.

These were hard times for us. In the morning, when my mother dropped me off at a kindergarten, she deposited my little half-brother in a nursery. After work she picked him up and did the shopping. I had to come home by myself, even though I was only four years old. But we really had no choice.

One day when I came home I found a guard armed with a huge rifle sitting in the middle of our living room. He had brought my stepfather home for a brief visit! As he had never seen his son, my stepfather had managed to persuade the warden to let him out for a few hours. At the time of the baby's birth, he had already been under arrest and had been sentenced and jailed without ever seeing his son. Mother treated the guard to vodka and he got quite drunk. I remember everyone being happy. After they left, our lives assumed their drabness.

I did love school. My childhood and youth were spent in the official system of the Soviet organizations. After kindergarten came the school and the Pioneer Camp, and then the university. I eventually became a dentist. Those students who did well academically were singled out for many honors, but those who misbehaved or performed poorly were publicly shamed. Public shame is a popular method of education in the Soviet Union. It is used on students and even adults, and we were all very concerned with our performance. The schools' atmosphere was very strict and quite puritanical.

In 1949 there was a new wave of arrests. They called it *"Zolotucha"* from the Russian word *Zoloto* (gold). It was believed that people were hiding gold in their homes, and the secret police searched houses, tearing up walls and floors. Mother had hidden letters from relatives and friends who lived in England and in Israel. Knowing that such letters would be considered treason, she burned them. In this way, we lost contact with all those people, and we were very unhappy.

That year my father was released from jail. He tried to help mother with my care and he came every week to take me out. I loved being with him, since he took me to puppet shows, to the circus, the ballet, and the cinema. He always seemed to be so carefree, and he set up a little bachelor apartment for himself on Valny Iela.

In 1952, my stepfather was released. He had a difficult time getting a job at first and therefore helped my mother with painting handkerchiefs. Eventually though, he got a job in a cooperative, where he manufactured paint. With two parents working, our lives became easier as far as economics was concerned, but once again there was a wave of anti-Semitism. Jewish physicians were the main target and the newspapers were full of their "crimes." They were accused of conspiring to poison the leading members of the Communist party. It was labeled by the government the "Doctors' Plot."

People were afraid to talk and my parents would fall silent when I came into their room. They worried that I might repeat what they had said and I was reminded never to tell anyone about what I had heard at home. In fact, this habit has remained with me to this day.

The doctors' trial was discontinued in March 1953, when Stalin died. I remember I was at school when the news of his death was broadcast.

All the students were supposed to cry—it was expected that we would feel sad—but as hard as I tried, I could not force a single tear. Somehow, my parents had succeeded in instilling a set of values that was contrary to the make-believe I was taught in school. It seems that even at a young age, I had realized that whatever was taught by the propaganda system of the Soviet Union was not to be trusted or believed, since most of it was only brainwashing used by people to advance their careers and secure their jobs.

It was clear that my mother groomed me for a different life, a life she herself had known before the war. Although religious holidays were not celebrated within the socialist system, in our home we always celebrated Rosh Hashana and Passover. Yom Kippur was observed by older people.

As a Jew, I was often singled out for insults by my schoolmates. Those who did not know that I was Jewish, especially at the university, often confided their anti-Semitic feelings to me. After all, I was as blond and blue-eyed as they were, so why not tell me about the "dirty" Jews?

It was very hard for me to trust people under these circumstances; yet there were some friends in my life, friends I had made very early through my cousin Lalia, whom I trusted from the very beginning. I met them in 1950 and all of our lives took very strange turns as we grew older.

There was, for instance, Margarita Solomiak. She married Vladimir Kuznetzov, who was condemned to death in 1968 by the Soviets for trying to hijack a plane to Israel. Owing to Western political pressure, he was pardoned and spent ten years in Siberia.

Then there was Sylvia Zalmanson, another good friend. She spent nine years in Siberian camps for belonging to the Zionist movement and for trying to escape to Israel.

Lalia, my cousin, almost became a runaway child after her mother, my Aunt Sonia, died and her father married the housekeeper.

In retrospect, I was the lucky one. Although I became a dissident and a refusenik, and fought to get out of the Soviet Union, I did not experience the brutal treatment my friends had to suffer. I managed to go to Israel, I got married, I brought up children, and I came to New York after the death of my second husband to start a new life.

That is what happened to all four of us. But way back in 1950, when we played our childish games, not one of us could imagine what the future would bring.

I dedicate this story to my grandparents and to all the other members of my family who were murdered by the Nazis. I have experienced the pattern of tragedy and pain, but I have learned that one should never lose hope in oneself, in one's family, and in one's beliefs.

EDITOR'S NOTE

Julia Robinson, now a film producer who lives in New York City, travels all over the world. She, her first husband Dr. Mark Libman, and their son, Daniel, left Riga in 1971. They joined her mother, who had left in 1965, after divorcing her stepfather. He died in Riga, in 1980, but Julia's natural father came to America in 1986.

Julia's second husband, Myles Robinson of Winnipeg, Canada, left her a widow; she raised his children with the same zest she brought to all her endeavors, be it getting a doctorate in dentistry, being a dissident and a refusenik in Russia, or producing a docudrama on Cambodia!

She opted for calling her vignette "Julia's Story" and I agreed. If I had my way, I would have called it "The Unsinkable Julia Robinson."

4

A Farm Called Jungfernhof

Trudy Ullmann Schloss

I was born in the town of Pforzheim in the German State of Baden. Although Hitler had been in power since 1933, it was only in April 1938 that I realized what it meant to be a Jew in Germany. On a lovely spring day, the director of the girls' high school I attended announced from the podium to the assembled student body that the three Jewish girls currently attending Hilda School would henceforth not be permitted to attend and would have to leave immediately. I was absolutely devastated.

Although I transferred to a makeshift Jewish school, it was never the same, and then in November the Nazis blew up Pforzheim's synagogue, shattered the windows of Jewish shops, and I had to watch helplessly as a few hoodlums beat my father, Sally Ullmann, to a pulp and nearly killed him. After this tragic event my parents felt that I should immediately learn a trade that would be useful for future emigration. My mother, Frieda Ullman, found out that the Jewish Hospital in Berlin accepted girls as young as fourteen as nursing students, since the shortage of Jewish nurses was such that it had to be alleviated. Under Nazi law, Jews could no longer be cared for by Aryan nurses and so, after sending in my application, I was accepted and on my way to Berlin.

We all thought that our tearful good-bye was only temporary. However, I was never to see my parents again. They were among the first

Jews to be deported from Germany. It was in October 1940, when my mother called me in Berlin to tell me that she, my father, and my younger sister Erna, were to go to France, to a concentration camp called Gurs. She sent me a postcard from the railroad station in which she indicated that the State of Baden would soon be *judenrein,* cleansed of Jews, and where she expressed the hope that we would one day be together again.

I found out in late 1945 that my mother had been sent to Auschwitz in September 1942 and that my father followed her in July 1943, after having spent some time in a camp called Rivesaltes. Both of them perished in Auschwitz and so did most of the Jews from Baden, Jews whose presence in that state could be traced back a thousand years.

My sister Erna survived. She was taken into a French convent, given a new name, and went to school. She now lives in New York.

I continued with my nursing course, at all times in touch with my relatives. My grandmother, Hannah Ullmann, lived in Stuttgart. In late 1942 she was sent to Theresienstadt and from there to Auschwitz, where she was gassed. In Haigerloch, a small town near Stuttgart, I had two uncles, both brothers of my father. Uncle Siegfried had come back from America several years earlier. He had lived there for many years, but after he lost his wife, he came back to Germany and married my Aunt Lilly. Uncle Louis, Aunt Jettchen, and their daughter Grete were also writing to me, and in late fall of 1941 I received a letter from them, saying that they were to be resettled in the East.

Since they were the only family I had left, I decided to go with them and so I left Berlin for Haigerloch in November. In looking back, I am certain that this decision saved my life, since only about a year later the patients of the hospital in Berlin where I studied nursing, as well as their nurses and physicians, were sent to Auschwitz, where all of them were gassed upon arrival.

Nothing like this ever entered my mind that November of 1941. All I wanted was to be together with some of my family and not stay all alone in those uncertain and dangerous times.

As expected, my relatives and I left Haigerloch for Stuttgart. At an "assembly" point we were joined by many other Jews, both from Stuttgart itself as well as from surrounding towns. On December 1, 1941, twelve hundred of us boarded the regular, heated railroad cars, destination Riga. Traveling in this manner never even gave rise to a thought of being in mortal danger. On the contrary, whatever suspicions some of the clever ones among us may have had were dispersed.

Four days later we arrived at a railway station called Skirotava, on the outskirts of Riga, the capital of Latvia. It was bitter cold and we were made to walk about five kilometers, prodded by Latvian SS in a most brutal fashion, until we reached what must have been an estate at one time and was then a collection of barns and wooden shacks. The name of the village itself was Jumpramuize, but we were told that the camp was Jungfernhof.

We were not the first Jews to arrive there. Two days earlier a transport had arrived from Nürnberg, consisting of Jews from Würzburg and Fürth as well. Four days earlier, about fifty young men from a Berlin transport had stopped in Jungfernhof for a day and had then been taken to Salaspils. They must have just sat down to eat, for we found the food frozen on the plates.

Men and women were separated and housed in the stalls once used for cattle and horses. Young, single females like myself and my cousin were placed upstairs, in a former hayloft. Our SS men, both German and Latvian, used the large farmhouse not too far from the stalls and barns.

Three days later, there were two more transports. One was from Vienna and the other from Hamburg. The latter brought that city's chief rabbi, Joseph Carlebach.

There were now four thousand Jews in a space that could not even hold four hundred. Several kitchens were opened. . . . they were just large kettles, with a roof over the cooks' heads, one kettle for each group. People were freezing, people got ill, people were dying. A sick bay was established in one of the barns and I, having had nurses' training, was ordered to work there. There was little in the way of medication, since upon arrival all our luggage had been confiscated. It was also impossible to bury the dead, since the ground was frozen and the SS did not want to dynamite it as yet; they had Russian prisoners of war do so in the forest, but we did not know that at the time.

Rabbi Carlebach celebrated Hanukkah 1941 for the many children and for the adults. His message was clear: "Through all adversity, for the last two millenia, the Jewish people had prevailed and persevered. They would do so now too." It did not sound very realistic just then, but in his steadfast belief he managed to console us. I remember that he was never idle during those few months I knew him . . . he comforted the sick and the dying, and he was revered by all of us.

There was a Bar Mitzvah in early March. The boy had come with the Hamburg transport, and now the rabbi led his motley congregation in their fervent prayers. It was the very last Bar Mitzvah at which he officiated and it brought to an end an illustrious career. Only a few days later, on March 26, 1942, the rabbi, together with his family and another two thousand Jews, including my "American" Uncle Siegfried and Aunt Lilly, was sent to what they cynically called "Camp Dünamünde," but which was actually the Bikernieku Forest. The idea, of course, was to calm the people so that they would go quietly, and the inventor of this illusionary camp was *Obersturmfuehrer* Gerhard Maywald. At his trial in 1977, in Hamburg, he felt that by doing this, he had done a good deed!

Before that last big *Aktion,* however, there were several small transports that left Jungfernhof. Some went on open vans, others by bus, and still others were taken away in closed vans, which, rumor had it, were using the exhaust system to kill the people inside before they even got to the forest. Many of our young men were sent to Camp Salaspils, a horrible place from which only very few ever returned. Then there was the so-called miracle transport. It consisted of two hundred women who ended up in the Riga ghetto. They were elderly and, also according to rumors, were not meant to go to the ghetto at all. The driver of the first van (there were the usual four) apparently was new in this business and lost his way. The other vans followed and the convoy ended up in front of the ghetto's *Kommandantur.* Most of the women were sent to their deaths during the big *Aktion* in the ghetto on March 15, 1942, but I know at least two of the survivors, Mrs. Elizabeth Kaplan and her daughter Rita from the Hamburg transport. The young girl had received permission to go along with her mother when the latter was selected to go.

Some of these selections occurred at night and most of the time, when we saw those four open vans, we were very much afraid and tried to hide. There was no other miracle; the vans brought their cargo to the forest.

My Uncle Louis was very ill. Yet, whenever possible, he tried to work so as not to endanger himself. By now, we all realized that our only hope was to work and to endure. My aunt and Grete worked at several places, among them the "sewing" room, where clothes from the confiscated suitcases were repaired. Other women carried water in pails to the makeshift kitchens and laundry rooms. There was also a work detail separating dishes, which had evidently been brought along by the deportees and were now sorted according to value. The best items, be they dishes or clothing, were shipped to Germany. Other things were given to loyal Latvians. Very little was left for us, the true owners. Some people managed to "steal" something back and then barter it when going to Skirotava, where the rails had to be cleared of snow on a daily basis. The punishment was death but that did not matter; for all practical purposes it seemed that we were doomed anyway.

The *Kolonnenfuehrer* (work detail leaders) of the various *Kommandos* were Harry Kahn, Max Eichberg, and Heinz Alexander. The first camp elder was a Mr. Kleeman, but soon Jupp Levy of Stuttgart took over. It was rumored that he often cooperated with the SS, especially when selections were made. In his blustery way he made many enemies and was eventually murdered when he arrived at Kaiserwald. But that, too, was in the future.

The *Kommandant* of Jungfernhof was *Oberscharfuehrer* Rudolf Seck. During selections, when young sons or daughters wanted to go with their parents—obviously not realizing that they were slated for destruction—Seck usually did not permit them to go. Years later, at his trial, he felt that in this way he had "saved" many Jews and should therefore not be judged too harshly!

Other SS officers, also present at selections as well as on different occasions, which they called "parties," were *Obersturmbannfuehrer* Rudolf Lange, *Obersturmfuehrer* Gerhard Maywald and other SS men of lesser rank. Lange was clearly in charge. It was his idea to create a model farm on the grounds of the old estate. In fact, he even made us use an old airstrip to plant potatoes, beets, and some other vegetables. Up until that time, it was Maywald who used the airstrip for his small plane.

When spring of 1942 finally arrived, it became evident that of the more than four thousand German Jews who had come to Jungfernhof, only four hundred were still alive. We had been saved by a combination of luck and skills, with luck being the main factor.

Jungfernhof now became a true model farm, visited by many German officials who admired all the good things we coaxed from the sandy soil. They did not see the large mass grave in the middle of the potato field, where the six hundred victims of the first few months lay buried. The other three thousand found their last resting place either in Salaspils or in the Bikernieku Forest, where the graves are outlined with uneven stones, placed there by the Soviet Commission in October 1944.

Life on the farm stabilized. Most of us became physically hardened. My Uncle Louis, however, finally succumbed and died in August 1942. He had suffered from a severe pleurisy and unbearable pain of shingles. He was buried at the edge of the potato field, on a little rise.

While over three hundred of us worked in the fields, the others were in service position such as the kitchen—by now a real one—as well as for the SS right at our camp and at other sites in the city. Through them we were in loose contact with the ghetto inmates. Our outside *Kommandos* told us that we looked healthier than the ghetto people; fieldwork was evidently beneficial!

Not only were we a model farm, but the formerly dilapidated barns and huts were clean and well kept. Where there had been an enormous pile of torn and ugly suitcases and satchels were now green plants.

These suitcases that we had brought, as well as many that came with subsequent transports which never reached the ghetto, were transferred to *Kommando* Lenta, situated at first in the city and later at the other side of the Daugava River. Our people had unloaded them at the station and brought them to Jungfernhof. Getting to their contents, although punishable by death, had been our only means to get items to barter for food. Now, of course, owing to the transfer, our bartering days were over and we had to make do with insufficient rations. But being on a farm, if we were adept, there were always home-grown vegetables.

Then, in early summer of 1943, after a year of relative quiet and stability, the authorities decided that half of us were expendable, myself, my aunt, and cousin Grete included. The other half was to stay at Jungfernhof until August 1944. Many of them were skilled artisans, but there were still many who worked in the fields. And when those were not enough, as for instance at harvest time in 1943, young men, both Latvian and German Jews, were brought from other work details, from the ghetto, and from Kaiserwald to work at the so-called *"Kartoffel Kommando."*

Right after they finished the harvest, their work became far more sinister. Most of them never returned to the places they had come from, but were put in chains and taken to the forests around Riga, where they had to dig up the corpses buried there, burn them, and then were killed and burned themselves. The *Kommando* was called *"Stuetzpunkt"* in Riga; its *Kommandant* was Eduard Roschmann. Since these young men were not permitted to live longer than two weeks, more and more were periodically selected both at the then almost empty ghetto and at Kaiserwald. Although there were many rumors, it took all of us a long time until we believed the awful truth.

In the meantime, though, the expendable half had landed in the Riga ghetto. My aunt and Grete remained there, as part of the Bielefeld group, but after only a few days I was sent to the peat bogs of Smarden, where I met my future husband Lewis Schloss. After Smarden we went to Hasenpot (Aizpute) and Plotzen near Libau (Liepaja) and then in October 1943 we were sent back to the Riga ghetto. It was a different ghetto from the one I had first seen only a few months earlier. For one thing, there were few people left. They had been taken to Kaiserwald and I, too, left for that awful place just days before the ghetto was liquidated.

At Kaiserwald, after a frightening reception, as I stood on roll call that first evening, a true miracle occurred, which helped me to survive the approaching winter. The blond SS woman who was in charge of the women's camp, Eva Kowa, was strutting back and forth, counting her charges, when her glance fell on me. She looked at me closely, looked again, and finally asked if I was Trudy Ullmann from Pforzheim. "Yes, I am," I replied, unsure of her motives. "Don't you recognize me?" she asked, and I said truthfully, "No, I don't." Frustrated by my lapse of memory, she told me that she had been a salesgirl in the Jewish shoestore in Pforzheim, at Schauer's, and had often sold shoes to my mother, my sister, and me.

She was quite happy about our "reunion," but it was I who had cause to be happy, for from that day on she watched over me. She was known as a brutal guard, but as far as I was concerned, she considered me "her" Jew and so she brought me food, right into the barracks, and even gave me a part of her own Christmas parcel from home on December 24, 1943. She also got me a job at the camp's clothing depot, where I was protected from the bitter cold and had ample opportunity to "liberate" or "organize" some clothes, which could then be bartered for food.

Then, in April 1944, it was Eva Kowa who helped me to secure a transfer from Kaiserwald to the HKP *(Heeres Kraftfahr Park)* where Lewis worked as an auto mechanic.

It was to be our last summer in Riga. When the Soviet Army was only about one hundred miles away from the city, the Germans did not want to let go of their victims, and after one last selection in every camp, at the end of July 1944, they took us "home to the *Reich,"* which for us meant the notorious concentration and extermination camp Stutthof near Danzig (Gdańsk).

On Sunday, August 6, 1944, as I entered the hold of the boat that was to carry us across the Baltic Sea and back to Germany, I saw several familiar faces, faces of the girls who had been with me in Jungfernhof! It seemed only natural that we tried and, for the most part, succeeded in staying together for the next few months, which were to sap all our strength and tax us to the utmost.

In Stutthof I met my Aunt Jettchen and my cousin Grete for the last time; they perished there. Thus, it turned out that I was the only one of my family to survive.

Together with five hundred women, most of them Hungarian, I was sent to a labor camp, called Sophienwalde, where I helped to build an important road. We used to joke that this road would facilitate the Soviet army's entry into the little town.

Of the four hundred men and women who were left alive at Jungfernhof in the spring of 1942, approximately fifty survived the war. I met some of them when I returned to Stuttgart in 1945. We are still in contact with each other and the bonds that were formed in our youth can never be broken.

I would like to thank my husband Lewis for prodding me to write the story of Jungfernhof and for having kept a letter I wrote in July 1945, where I mentioned many details that I later forgot or made myself forget.

I would also like to thank Hannelore Marx, nee Kahn, Stuttgart transport, and Gerda Wasserman, nee Rose, Hamburg transport, for helping me refresh my memory when I wanted to describe the events of that time.

I was told that there is no sign at the village of Jumpramuize, and that very few Latvians in the vicinity remember the German Jews who grew all those good vegetables. We, the survivors, on the other hand, have not forgotten; we remember the people we lost and as long as we live none of us will ever cease to remember the model farm called "Jungfernhof."

EDITOR'S NOTE

I first met Trudy Ullmann in Kaiserwald, and I used to marvel at the special relationship she had with the dreaded SS woman Eva Kowa. Then, on the *Bremerhafen,* the boat that took us to Danzig (Gdańsk), I met Trudy again, and through her some of the girls from the famous model farm at Jungfernhof.

Eventually, after a series of traumatic events, we ended up at the labor camp Sophienwalde, described in chapter one, where Trudy Ullmann almost lost her arm to an infection brought about by a bite—a human bite—sustained during a fight over a blanket. It was the Viennese camp physician who cut the ugly, festering wound with a pocketknife, and thus saved Trudy's arm and most certainly her life. The same doctor nursed her through an eight-week bout with typhoid fever.

Shortly after the war, Trudy married her boyfriend Lewis, and when they arrived in the United States one year later, she went back to her profession of nursing.

Trudy and Lewis have a son and a daughter. Now that they are retired and their children have long since left the house, Trudy and Lewis serve as volunteers on the sick wards of a major hospital in New Jersey. In addition, both of them address students of all ages as well as congregations and tell them about the Holocaust.

At this time, Trudy's nursing talents are used for a very special and delightful purpose: She and Lewis became grandparents and their happiness is complete!

5

The Jewish SS Officer

Elke Sirewitz, Son of Yankel and Sore Sirewitz, Also Known as Obersturmfuehrer Fritz Scherwitz

Alexander Levin
(Translated from Russian by Liuba Rakhman)

I have worked on this story for many years and I still feel that it reads like a movie script. It is so phantastic that the head of Yad Vashem in Israel could not believe it until I brought him the documents and the notes I had made after interviewing eyewitnesses. But all of it is true, and Elke, alias Fritz, was a phenomenon such as occurs only very seldom.

On August 10, 1910, Sore Sirewitz felt that her time had come and sent for the midwife, well known in the tightly knit Jewish community of Vilno (Vilnius).

Since this was not her first such experience, Sore gave birth easily to a little boy, whom they called Elias, or Elke for short. The day of Elke's circumcision fell on the ninth of Ab, a sad day for Jews, for it was on that day that the Holy Temple in Jerusalem had been destroyed by the Romans.

In the light of Elke's future life, with all its strange twists and turns, the date might have been symbolic.

Elke's father Yankel was a failure. Whatever he undertook turned against him, and always for the worse. The only thing at which he was successful was begetting children, and in accordance with his religious duties, he fulfilled the behest of the Jewish laws "to go and multiply."

While several children died in infancy, three brothers and one sister grew to adulthood.

The Sirewitz family lived in abject poverty. No matter what he did, Yankel never succeeded in feeding or dressing his family. With the outbreak of World War I, the conditions worsened. At the time, Elke was just four years old.

In 1915, Vilno was occupied by the Germans. In comparison to the various occupations throughout the past centuries, the Germans behaved rather decently vis-à-vis the Jewish population. Although Vilno had been called the "Lithuanian Jerusalem," its Jews had suffered grievously through military actions, epidemics, fires, pogroms, depressions, persecutions, and witch hunting. Yet, despite all of this, it had become an important center of Jewish spiritual and cultural life.

There was a great strength in this Jewish community, a strength that was honed in the course of centuries; it became part of individuals and there is no doubt that little Elke Sirewitz inherited some of this strength and eventually exhibited it in rather peculiar ways.

In 1917 Yankel Sirewitz moved his family from Vilno to Šiauliai (Schaulen in German and Shavli in Russian), a little town one hundred miles northwest of Vilno. He felt he would be able to make a better living there. While this was only a dream, and their poverty continued, their life was a quiet one there and it was more stable than it had been in Vilno.

The reason for this may have been the fact that the Germans continued their presence there. The German *Freikorps* Regiment had its quarters at Šiauliai, commanded by *General Feldmarschall* von der Goltz. The combat mission of the regiment was to fight against the communist influence and the penetration of the Soviets into the Baltic States.

Little Elke, in order to contribute something to the family's strained circumstances, started working in the kitchen of the regiment and never failed to bring food to his parents and his siblings. The bright, charming boy was considered "the son of the regiment" and the kindhearted soldiers of the *Freikorps* called him "little Moses." Šiauliai's German police commissioner Fritz Erler took to calling Elke "Fritz" and people got used to it. Erler saw to it that little Fritz was clean, that he was well clothed, and that his German became fluent, without a Jewish inflection. He became the boy's protector to such an extent that he asked Yankel and Sore to let the boy join the regiment when it was clear that it would become a mobile unit.

Elke's parents made their decision with heavy hearts. They knew that their son's only chance for a better life was in leaving Šiauliai, but to let him go with a non-Jew and a soldier at that, was a little too much. However, when Erler promised that he would take good care of the boy, that he would take him into his home and give him a good education, they decided to let him go.

They knew Erler as a good and decent man and they also felt that eventually peace would come to the region once more and Elke would then come back to them. Thus, for the time being, they let Elke go with Erler, always with the hope that he would return some day.

Erler got papers for Elke, added some years to his age, and took him to Lower Silesia with him. Evidently due to a clerk's error, the papers were made out to "Fritz Scherwitz" and Erler never let on to anyone that his "godson" Fritz was of Jewish origin.

Erler, now a civilian, took care of Fritz's elementary education and after some time sent him to Berlin, where Fritz became a student at a vocational school, run by the Siemens factory, specializing in precision mechanics and instrument making. Thanks to his native intelligence, his aptitude for mechanics, his self-determination, and diligence, Fritz became an outstanding student. In addition, he was very interested in sports and made a name for himself as a well-known amateur wrestler. Whenever Erler came to see him, he was happy. He called him "uncle" and both of them were careful never to mention his origins.

In 1931, when he turned twenty-one in accordance with his true date of birth, he decided to pay a visit to his family in Šiauliai. He was shocked by their poverty, he felt sorry for his sick mother, whose leg had turned lame, he was impatient with his parents' trust in God when it seemed to him that help from that quarter was obviously not forthcoming, and he knew he could not stay. In a depressed state of mind, he returned to Berlin.

Within the next two years, great changes were to take place in Germany. The aged Hindenburg appointed Hitler *Reichskanzler*, and the populace was jubilant. Whether it was because of the general euphoria, or whether it was because of his wish to stay with his club as an amateur wrestler, Fritz Scherwitz decided to join the SS. On November 1, 1933, he received SS number 241935, and was now truly a part of the Third Reich.

His position was actually fraught with dangers; he must have been aware of the regime's anti-Jewish policies. Yet, he was a rather calculating person and when he joined the SS, he had used the documents he had received thanks to Erler and the *Freikorps*. Somehow, because of a fortuitous set of circumstances, he managed to avoid the obligatory proof of his "pure" ancestry. The deception was successful, and there was no stopping him.

He rose rapidly in the world of business. At first, he was promoted within Siemens, but pretty soon he was offered the position of director at the Hermersdorfer Werke in Berlin. In 1938 he was married, and his wife bore him a daughter only a year later. They named the baby Rosemarie. It was quite clear to him that there was no way anyone could ever find out about his true past. He would see to it that his life would be a good one, no matter what. Erler had died by then, so there was no witness left. Only his family knew his secret, but they were far away!

In 1939, when war broke out, Fritz Scherwitz was called to arms. As a member of the Second Battalion of the Anti-Aircraft Police, he took part in the short campaign against Poland. We can only wonder what impact the treatment meted out to the Jews in Poland had on him. Earlier, of course, while still in Berlin, he was a witness to the *Kristallnacht* events of November 9, 1938, when all of Berlin's synagogues were destroyed. How did he feel? What went through his mind? We shall never know.

A few weeks after the Polish campaign, Fritz returned to Berlin, but not for long. In June 1941, he joined the One Hundred Thirty-First Police Battalion and went East once more.

His unit moved through Tilsit (Sovetsk), Riga, and Pleskau (Pskov). At the battle of Tallinn (Reval) in October 1941, he sustained a wound in the leg and was transferred to a military hospital in Riga. The wound was not a serious one, and anyone else would have returned to the front. But not Fritz Scherwitz. He was evidently not willing to be a hero and when he met an old acquaintance of his from Berlin, who happened to be attached to the SD (the dreaded *Sicherheits Dienst*), Fritz obtained the help he had been looking for. He was transferred to the SD headquarters in Riga and became a driver there; although the job was low in prestige or power, it kept him away from the front.

The winter of 1941–42 was extremely severe. One night, during a snowstorm, Fritz's car broke down. While waiting to be rescued, he suffered severe frostbite on both feet. After his feet healed, he was not assigned to driving a car but became "officer of the watch," joining a unit that consisted of SS men who escorted Jews walking to and from the ghetto to their jobs in the city. Fritz was assigned to the work detail of those Jews who were employed in the Gestapo workshops at headquarters.

Based on what we know about Fritz up to that time, we must assume that he had been looking for a job that would bring him into contact with Jews. Furthermore, we must also assume that he wanted to help them—if at all possible and without danger to himself.

Although he knew perfectly well that a visit to his family might prove disastrous, he risked it anyway, since the distance between Šiauliai and Riga was only sixty miles. He may have wanted to help them; as he was to say many years later, he actually wanted to take them out of the ghetto there. All he could do at the time, however, was to give his sister Rivka some food. He did not have the power he would get later. Rivka told him that his father and one of his brothers had left for America in 1933. She and her husband, as well as Elke's mother and the other brother, were in the Šiauliai ghetto. Her girlfriend, Fanny Papiermeister, who had been a neighbor before the ghetto was established, had known Elke as a boy and was aghast when she saw him in the hated uniform. She was sworn to secrecy.

Scherwitz managed to see Rivka several more times, always leaving food with her. Many years later, in Israel, her girlfriend related how Rivka was ostracized by the other ghetto inmates who saw her with Elke. They had no idea that he was her brother, but thought she was his girlfriend. (Although relations between Aryans and Jews were strictly forbidden, the ghettos and even camps in the East had a good deal of these dangerous liaisons.)

In August 1944, when the ghetto of Šiauliai was liquidated, about half of its inhabitants were killed in the forests and the other half, among them the members of Elke's family, were sent to Stutthof. Sore Sirewitz died in Stutthof; Rivka and her girlfriend were sent to a work camp, as were her husband and her brother. Eventually, authorities at the women's camp found out that Rivka and two other women were pregnant. They were sent to Dachau and were killed there by injection. Fanny, Rivka's girlfriend, survived and went to Israel after the war. Elke's brother survived too and went to America in 1946, presumably to find his father and other brother. Rivka's husband survived and came to Israel as well.

Back in Riga in early 1942, the workshops at the Gestapo experienced a drastic change with the arrival of German, Austrian, and Czech Jews who were being deported to the East. Their suitcases were brought to the workshops, and their belongings were sorted according to value. The very best items were sent to Germany, the mediocre clothing and other things were given to loyal Latvians, and only the rags were given back to the Jews. With these, they could replace whatever clothing they had worn until it fell apart.

It was at that time, in early 1942, that Scherwitz ceased to be an escort of Jews. He saw to it that all those artisans were housed right in the city, near the workshops, and that he was put in charge of them. We can only surmise that he knew the right people to effect such a change in procedure and that he knew how to make them beholden to him. His rank was still rather low.

As more transports arrived, he added more workers to his force. Since many of the deportees never reached the Riga ghetto, but were murdered in the nearby forests, still other additional work had to be done. The hapless victims had to take off their clothes before being shot, and therefore quite a lot of cleaning and repairing had to be done, in addition to separating everything into three groups.

The loot was incredible! The jewelry and money found in the pockets was worth a fortune! And Scherwitz had access to all of it! Even after transferring much of the loot to Germany, enough was left to be used for bribes, establishing connections, and simply for good living.

According to survivors' diaries and reports, Scherwitz was very good to "his" Jews. He made one of them, Boris Rudow, the head of the workers and later got him papers that indicated that he was not a Jew, but a Russian; he could now go freely in and out of Lenta, notwithstanding that Rudow's father and two brothers were right there in the camp.

When the space at Gestapo Headquarters proved inadequate, Scherwitz requisitioned an old factory at the other side of he River Daugava and installed the whole *Kommando* Lenta there. By now there were four hundred Jews busy with all kinds of jobs. High officials of the SD and Gestapo came to Lenta to have their uniforms and clothes made by craftsmen. Scherwitz thus assured himself of their support, should he ever have need for it. He tried to show that the Lenta Jews could do any job. He made Rudow his assistant and put Schoenberger in charge of the Jews.

In comparison to all the other camps in Riga, Lenta was really exceptional. All of this was due to Scherwitz. The Jews had food, they had excellent quarters, and many were together with their families. Max Kaufmann, in his opus *Die Vernichtung der Juden Lettlands* (the destruction of Latvian Jewry), reports how Scherwitz warned everyone before other SS or SD came to check on them and how good the life in Lenta was when compared to the other outside camps. Gertrude Schneider in *Journey Into Terror: The Story of the Riga Ghetto* calls Lenta "a veritable paradise."

Although Scherwitz's wife came to visit him from Berlin, he had a girlfriend among the Jewish women at Lenta. Her name was Tamara Sherman, called "Esther" by her fellow Jews. Eventually, after attempts had been made by other SS to get rid of her, Scherwitz realized that her position had become dangerous; they could do very little to him, but they could hurt him through her. Everyone knew that he was very fond of her. He retaliated by getting forged papers for her and took her to Paris, where she survived the war.

When he returned from Paris, Scherwitz brought back perfume, champagne, and cognac for his cronies. According to Gerda Gottschalk's unpublished memoirs *"Der Letzte Weg,"* he did this several times. Gottschalk spent a few months in Lenta, and while she gets Scherwitz's rank wrong, she is correct in her description of the camp.

In the summer of 1944, terrible news reached the Jews at the Lenta compound. Selections were held at all camps in the vicinity! Once again, there was much activity in the forests! Furthermore, a transport of over two thousand German, Latvian, and Lithuanian Jews, as well as several thousand Hungarian Jews so recently brought to Riga, had been sent away by boat.

In order to forestall a selection at Lenta, Scherwitz transferred the majority of his charges, many of whom were vulnerable, to camp Salaspils. At that time, Salaspils was a camp for Russians and Latvians only.

The Lenta contingent stayed there for one week and after they came back safely, several of the men went to Scherwitz and proposed that at the last moment they would all go out to meet the Red Army, which was approaching rapidly, and would "intercede" for him.

He was visibly touched, thanked them, and then calmed them down, saying that there was no need to leave just yet. He assured them of his continued support, but not everyone wanted to listen. Several men decided to escape. Among them were Hirsch Schenker, Edgar Heidt, Erich Hirschfeld, and Moshe Glazer.

Unfortunately, they were caught, brought back to Lenta, and shot. It will probably never be known for certain who shot them. Was it Scherwitz himself? Was he afraid that they knew too much? Did he have to shoot them in order to show the other SS men that he was truly one of theirs? And if he did not shoot them, would it not be logical to assume that it was done on his orders? The situation was chaotic all over, and Lenta was no exception.

The order to leave came in September 1944, and the majority of Lenta's Jews left Riga by boat. They and the last remnant of Jews from Kaiserwald were brought to the concentration and extermination camp

Stutthof, where they arrived on October 1, 1944. Not too many survived the following winter.

Scherwitz, having received special orders, took eighty of his most skilled workers to Libau in Kurland, which was liberated the day the war ended, on May 9, 1945. By then not many were left. He had not been able to save them. Boris Rudow had fled and survived the war, but the Soviets put him on trial for collaboration with the enemy and sent him to Siberia for ten years. After serving his sentence, he settled in Riga. In 1972 he received permission to leave and made his way to Israel. When he arrived there, the survivors of Lenta carried him on their shoulders and honored him.

Scherwitz, in May of 1945, made his way to Germany. The Americans caught him and put him into a prisoner of war camp near Erfurt. With the help of some of his Lenta Jews he managed to flee and made his way to Bavaria, where he worked tirelessly to get back confiscated property for victims of the Nazis.

In 1948, on one of his frequent trips to Munich, Scherwitz ran into one of his Jews from Lenta, Schapiro, who told him that a book had just come out, written by Max Kaufmann, in which Lenta was mentioned favorably. According to Schapiro, Scherwitz wanted to meet Kaufmann and did so, never imagining that Kaufmann would then denounce him as a former SS man.

In these three years since the war had ended, the survivors of Lenta, some of whom were in Latvia, some who came to Israel, some who came to England and the United States, often spoke about Scherwitz and of how good he had been to them. They did not know what had become of him, except for the few who had remained in Germany. Then, one day, they heard that he had been arrested in Bavaria at the behest of Max Kaufmann and would have to stand trial for executing Schenker, Heidt, and one other, "nameless" Jew as a punishment for escaping Lenta. Nothing in the trial records was said about Hirschfeld and Glazer.

Then came the big surprise: Scherwitz was not Fritz Scherwitz at all, but Elke Sirewitz . . . a Jew! This, then, was the explanation of why he could sing Yiddish songs and why he had done so much for them! Nevertheless, the news split the survivors into two camps. There were those who felt that he had done his best to save as many as he possibly could, and there were those who felt that he had used them, had enriched himself, and had indeed murdered the three men who had tried to escape. Some of his detractors even thought that the three had received permission from him to escape and that he had to silence them.

The most damning evidence at the time came from people who had never even been at Lenta but were so blinded by their own suffering and their hatred of anything German that they did not behave in a rational manner. One of those testimonies came from one Rafael Schub, then living in Toronto, but the discrepancies it contained made it doubtful enough to be dismissed by the court. He attributed deeds and motives to Scherwitz that were incongruous and patently untrue, all of them hearsay, for Schub had never set foot in Lenta. On the other hand, the diary written by Lenta survivor A. Bloch, now deposited at Yad Vashem in Jerusalem, never mentioned any crimes committed by Scherwitz—on the contrary! Bloch had gone back to Riga in 1945 and found his diary in the canister where he had hidden it; thus, his words, in contrast to those of Schub, had the ring of truth to them. Too late to make any difference, but just for the record, in 1971 another survivor of Lenta, Bentsion Chaan, came forward and gave testimony to "set the record straight." He, too, found very little that he could blame Scherwitz for.

The main witness against Scherwitz, at his first trial, was a man by the name of Matyukov. None of the surviving Lenta Jews could remember him! He never came back for a second hearing, which occurred after Scherwitz had already been in prison near Augsburg. At that second trial, it was established that Scherwitz had never changed his name or his appearance after the war, had used his considerable talents to aid concentration camp victims, and had not feared any repercussions. The only thing he changed was his first name; he went back to Elias, or Elke, and he divorced his wife.

It was obvious that he suffered. He had lost his family in a way that he knew only too well, he had tried to help his fellow Jews only to be hated by some of them, and he was accused of having either executed or abetted the execution of three Jews who had fled, something he denied emphatically. The judges in Germany, considering Scherwitz's Jewish background, agreed that he had been under great emotional stress and acknowledged the special circumstances that must have led him to shoot the three escapees. Had they been put to torture and interrogations, they might have told the SD more than was good for Scherwitz. They sentenced him to six years in prison.

Scherwitz appealed three times. He asked to be confronted by Matyukov. Curiously, his appeal was denied each time, for Matyukov was not to be found. Even so, he had to serve his sentence and lost his civil rights.

Although the whole case was highly unusual, the news media in Germany hardly covered it. In Munich there was an article by H. J. Huber in the magazine *Echo der Woche* and there was a short note about the trial in the newspaper *Frankenpost* in Hof an der Saale. An article by N. Kliger, in the *Alef* magazine in Israel, was rather laudatory of Scherwitz.

In New York, however, *Aufbau,* a German weekly read mainly by refugees, published an article based on information given by Max Kaufmann, who had by then emigrated to the United States. It describes Scherwitz as the head of the Gestapo in Latvia, and Kaufmann describes how Scherwitz's wish to get a copy of his book got him arrested!

When that article is compared to what Kaufmann had originally written in his book, it seems rather questionable that he knew the whole truth. Yet, it was because of Kaufmann that Scherwitz was brought to trial, even though he called him Max instead of Fritz and had ostensibly been looking for him ever since his liberation.

The question I have been asking for many years is this: If Scherwitz was really guilty, and if he enriched himself to the extent some of the witnesses claimed he had, what was he doing in Germany and why would he go to Munich so often, knowing well that many of the Latvian Jews were living there? Furthermore, why would he take a job to help Jews get back their belongings? And why would he divorce his German wife?

It seems to me that he never did feel any guilt at all and had perhaps no real reason to feel guilty. This supposition is borne out by the testimony of people who worked under his rather benign rule at Lenta, people such as Maria Caspary, Bloch, Chaan, Werner Sauer, Gerda Gottschalk, Karl Schneider and others, most of whom could not come to the trial, having left Germany in 1946 or 1947.

I would say that he felt great sorrow about the death of his mother and sister and so many others of his people and that he felt secure in the thought that he had done his best to help at least a few of them.

Many years later, his daughter Rosemarie asked me, "Where were all of them when he needed them? He had helped them in their hour of need, but they did not!" What could I say to her? In my opinion, she was right.

At the time of his trial he was engaged to be married to a Jewish girl, also a survivor. She left for Israel shortly after he was arrested and incarcerated, and started a new life without him.

Scherwitz was in jail for the whole six years. After his release he tried to have the trial reopened in order to have the judgment changed. He was unsuccessful in his endeavors.

In 1955, he married a German woman, but he was quite ill for most of the seven years they were together. He died on December 4, 1962, at the age of fifty-two of a heart attack, and is buried in his wife's family tomb on the *Westfriedhof* of Munich.

He took many secrets of his eventful life with him, and we shall never know how he was able to fool the Germans into believing him to be of "pure" race when all along he was no other than Elke, the son of Yankel and Sore.

EDITOR'S NOTE

I met Alexander Levin twice; once in 1989, when he received an award, and then in 1990, when I examined the material he had collected over a period of sixteen years. We had corresponded earlier and I marveled at his zeal to find out in minute detail what had made Elke Sirewitz "tick." To my great surprise, there was more, much more, which threw light on the personality of Alexander and his obsession. He had published a book in 1986, in Israel, titled *In the Devil's Teeth,* a concise autobiography.

After surviving the ghetto of Riga, camps Kaiserwald, Spilve, Magdeburg, and a death march, Alexander was liberated by the Russians. That particular unit of the Soviet Army asked for someone who could speak both Russian and German. The fact that he was the only one who could sealed his subsequent fate. He was given a uniform, worked for them interrogating German prisoners, but was then accused of being an enemy of the Soviet Union and sent to Siberia's vast network of gulags.

After some harrowing experiences, he was permitted to go to his native Riga. There was a short-lived amnesty and he took advantage of it. His father, who had survived the war, was in Riga as well. Alexander got married and worked in the steel industry. At some time in the late fifties, he met Boris Rudow, who had returned to Riga in 1955. It may have been Rudow's wartime exploits that whetted Alexander Levin's curiosity about Scherwitz. He, his wife, and two sons left Riga in 1972— as did Rudow—leaving behind his father, who died there in 1975.

In Israel, Levin again turned to the making of steel. At the same time, he worked on his memoirs and also on the story of the enigma Scherwitz. In 1978, the German prosecutor asked Levin to testify against Major Victors Arajs, whose well-known death squads had been used to liquidate Latvia's Jews and whose members had then been sent to the various extermination centers. I was intrigued by Levin's comment, and I quote from his book, *In the Devil's Teeth:*

Judge Wagner asked me if I was related to Arajs by blood . . . indeed, there are ties of blood between the defendant and me . . . rivers of blood . . . the blood of my relatives who were killed by this monster. Perhaps it was he who killed my mother in the Rumbuli Forest? I just said "no" and kept my thoughts to myself. Then, Arajs's lawyer, Dr. Steinecker, tried to tell the court that the memory of someone like me, after a period of thirty-seven years has passed, is at best incomplete. He evidently could not understand that for me it is not a long time, it is something that happened just yesterday and it will always be yesterday, to the last day of my life. (Translated from Russian by Liuba Rakhman)

At this point in time, Alexander Levin is retired, his sons are active officers in the Israeli Army, and he is taking care of an extensive correspondence with friends all over the globe. All he is hoping for is a telephone call to appear as a witness against the Soviet camp commander Starodonov Petrov and other "comrades."

He has deposited the documents in regard to Scherwitz with Yad Vashem. I was able to speak with other Lenta survivors not interviewed by Levin, and Jack Ratz, a board member of the Jewish Survivors of Latvia, who was at Lenta for most of the time in question, writes, "It was Fritz Scherwitz who saved our lives—when he found that among the Jews there was one who squealed to his superiors, he told the other Jews and they took care of the guy! Whenever Scherwitz had to go out of town and we had someone else in charge, there were the inevitable shootings or hangings, just like at the other camps in the vicinity. But not when Scherwitz was there! Never!"

I then asked Jack Ratz why witnesses did not come forward to save Scherwitz. He said, and I agree, that 1948 and the next few years saw the Jews leave the Displaced Persons camps and go to either the United States or Israel. Very few stayed behind and those who did were never called as witnesses, nor did they read it in newspapers. Compared to "real" SS murders, Scherwitz's sentence was excessive. For instance, *Sturmbannfuehrer* Gerhard Maywald, who on February 5, 1942 selected 1,500 Jews from the Berlin and Vienna groups of the German ghetto in Riga to be killed at the Bikernieku Forest on that same day, was sentenced to four years in 1977 by that same Judge Wagner who conducted the Arajs trial. But then, Maywald was not a Jew!

It may well be that the judges in the Scherwitz case were upset that this man had tricked their own people, posing as an SS man, when he was nothing but a Jew. The sentence, in other words, was his punishment for not "knowing his place!"

6

The Death Sentence

Inge Berner

I was born and grew up in Berlin and lived with my parents Bruno and Flora Gerson and younger brother Herbert in a large, comfortable apartment in the center of town. Our neighbors were civil servants, merchants, and workers. Their children were our playmates. Many of my uncles, aunts, and cousins lived within walking distance, as did my beloved grandmother, Oma Bertha Opprower. I went to school just a few blocks from home, and when I entered the Margareten Lyzeum at age ten, I was just as proud as my classmates, wearing the school's insignia on my cap. There were four other Jewish girls in my class, and I do not think that any of us ever encountered anti-Semitism in that school.

My father had volunteered for service in the German army at the outbreak of World War I, had fought for *Kaiser und Vaterland,* was wounded and had received the Iron Cross. He was very proud of that and he attended every meeting of the Jewish War Veterans' organization. Both his and my mother's families had lived in Germany for many generations; they therefore considered themselves German and loved their country. At the same time, they were good Jews and all of us attended services at the local synagogue every Friday night, as well as most Saturdays and holidays.

I had a happy childhood and I remember the beautiful parties on the occasion of birthdays and anniversaries. I also remember the lovely summer days we spent at our little cottage on the Spree River, where my father kept a sleek canoe. During our long summer vacations, my brother and I went to the farm of our maid's parents in Pomerania. Little did I foresee that my experiences at that farm, such as milking cows, feeding the animals, bringing in the wheat harvest, would one day many years later made me volunteer at the notorious concentration camp Stutthof, when a call went out for "experienced farm workers." Being a farm worker that summer of 1944 may even have saved me from the typhus epidemic soon to break out and kill so many of my friends.

January 30, 1933, brought an end to life as I had known it until then. With Hitler's rise to power we were suddenly outcasts. Neighbors who had always greeted us with a friendly "Good Morning," hardly looked at us anymore. The house porter, who had always been "Karl" to us, now insisted on being called "Herr Horstmann;" he was one of the first men in our district to sport the swastika emblem on his lapel.

The same ugly insignia also appeared on the lapel of our homeroom teacher, who told us that the Jewish girls were to sit in back of the room from now on. There were, however, a number of teachers who made it a point to be extra nice to us, especially our French teacher, Mrs. Else Koven. We were no longer asked to participate in extracurricular school activities and finally my parents decided—after much discussion with the other Jewish parents—to take me out of that school and enroll me in a Jewish school, a good thirty minutes' walk from home. Most of the time I took the trolley and I was not too upset by the change, since the new school was located right next door to where my Oma Bertha lived. I spent many hours in her room at the old age home and even received permission to sleep over on Friday nights, so that I could go to the synagogue with her on Saturday mornings.

The school was an old one. It had first been a boys' school and then a girls' school, which my mother and my Aunt Dorothea attended. In fact, my teacher, Miss Klara Heilmann, had been my mother's teacher too. (Miss Heilmann's brother was the famous Social Democrat Ernst Heilmann. He was held prisoner in a concentration camp almost from the beginning of the Nazis' rise to power and was executed in 1940.)

After some time had passed, the school became coeducational. Since state and private schools were expelling their Jewish students, our classrooms were packed with over sixty children each, children from all walks of life. There were some who were brought to school in chauffeured limousines from the posh Western parts of Berlin, and there were others who came from the poorest sections, almost like ghettos, where I had never been before and which seemed to me quite exotic, with Hebrew lettering on storefronts and the sound of Yiddish spoken by my new schoolmates' parents.

We did have wonderful teachers. They had been forced, just as we had been, to leave their posts at prestigious schools all over Berlin, but now, since the administration had the pick of the crop, we were really lucky to be taught by these outstanding personalities.

I especially remember our music teacher, Mr. Alfred Loewy, a small intense man who drilled music into our heads. To this day, whenever I attend an opera or a concert, I can hear his voice explaining the structure of music. We often played tricks on him, and I can only now imagine how he must have been annoyed by these little monsters who did not share his love for music.

Since all of us were in the same boat, we formed special friendships without restraints. My dearest friends were Charlotte Arpadi and Caroline Rules, and they have remained so until this very day. Two others were Marianne Prager and Hilde Loewy, each of whom was to die a heroine's death as resistance fighters against the Nazis.

Marianne and I joined a youth group, the BDJJ, *Bund Deutscher Juedischer Jugend,* a liberal, German-oriented (even at that time!) organization, which eventually turned into a resistance group. Of course, we were then much too young to do anything beyond holding discussions and reading forbidden books at first. Later, when all these youth groups—and there were many, especially Zionist ones—were no longer permitted to exist, our group went underground. We still had meetings but no longer in public places, only in private homes.

School life became normalized. Classes became smaller as many students and teachers too emigrated to other countries. The quality of our education, however, remained on the same high level. Somehow we knew that we had to learn more, not only academic but practical subjects as well.

Although we realized that Germany could no longer be our home, owing to the increasing pressure, my father felt that he had fought for his country, had been wounded, had always been a good German and that therefore nothing really bad would happen to us. Even when he lost his business, even when a Nazi big shot forced us to give up our apartment to him, even when family members left Germany and urged us to do likewise, my father said no.

Owing to my friendships at school and our tightly knit group of young people, we were able to have a semblance of a normal teenage life. We met in each other's houses for dancing and singing, we went on outings,

and every so often we sneaked into opera houses and theaters, although
this was strictly forbidden for Jews. We did have a Jewish theater too,
with first rate actors and actresses, all of whom were forced out of their
previous engagements at German institutions.

Looking for something more challenging, Marianne and I became more
involved with the illegal youth group. I left it after a while, since I
could not agree with the totally atheistic view of the leaders. I did keep
up my friendship with Marianne though. Caroline left for the United
States, crying all the way because she was an ardent Zionist and had
wanted to go to Palestine. Sometime later, Charlotte, her brother, and
their parents, left for Riga, Latvia, where they were to await their turn
for a visa to the United States. We corresponded regularly, and when
Charlotte met her future husband and was forbidden by her parents to
have any contact with him, she enclosed a letter for him with her letter
to me and I sent it to him. His letters in turn came to me and I sent
them to Charlotte.

This was the first time that the name Riga became more familiar to
me than just a word in a geography lesson. Charlotte's descriptions of
this medieval town sounded lovely and her secret romance made it even
more intriguing. I had no idea at all that I would see that city one day—
although not from a very good vantage point.

In April 1938 all of us except Caroline had graduated from our school
with the *Reifezeugnis,* the certificate of *matura,* but there was no way
for a Jew to continue his education at a college or a university. I therefore looked for a job. In my last year at school, I had taken a business
course and I applied at a number of Jewish businesses. (Any non-Jewish
firm would not have hired me and even if they had, I would not have
felt at ease.) I soon found employment in the Berlin garment center,
which was still, as it had always been, in Jewish hands. Although many
owners and workers had left Germany, there were still quite a number
of them left.

I worked for K. Messerschmidt, a small dress manufacturing business
in the older part of Berlin. I was the only one in the office and Mr.
Messerschmidt was a strict taskmaster. I learned a great deal from him
about running an office. His partner, who was also the firm's bookkeeper, was a Gentile woman and just as stern as Mr. Messerschmidt;
both of them saw to it that I was busy from eight in the morning until
six in the evening, six days a week. But I was young and I still managed
to have time for my friends. We got together in each other's homes for
discussions and also for fun like dancing and singing the latest hit songs.
Some of us had the forbidden American "swing" records. My cousin

Erich Gerson acted as my chaperone, since he was a year older than I, but there was little opportunity for more than just harmless entertainment.

On November 9, 1938, I went to work as usual. I did not see anything out of the ordinary, except for the fact that Mr. Messerschmidt was absent. Also, the telephone rang more often than usual and the bookkeeper always rushed to answer it, even though that was really one of my duties. It was getting dark rather early that day and in late afternoon I heard the sounds of glass breaking. Looking out the window, I saw a mob of people smashing the store window of a candy shop owned by an old Jewish couple. The man had a beard; he was forced down to his knees and made to brush the street with it. The people around him laughed and howled with glee.

One of the girls from our shipping department came running into the office and said to me, "Go home quickly, and use the back streets." I did as she told me and as I knew the old historic neighborhood very well from the many Sunday outings with my father, I got home without encountering any more mobs. My parents and my brother were already home; we closed the blinds and drew the curtains. The telephone kept ringing; the news was terrible. Relatives had been arrested and taken away. Several synagogues were burning but we did not hear any fire engines.

There was a light knock on our door and when my father looked through the peephole, he saw our former maid Martha Fechner, now Loebl. In 1935, after many years of service, she had been forced to leave us, as German women were no longer permitted to work for Jews. After leaving us, she had gotten married and now had a little girl, Christl, whom we all adored. She had never lost contact with us and had now come to take my father with her, so that she could hide him in her husband's workshop. Father did not want to go, but we urged him and after a few more alarming phone calls, he finally consented.

This terrible night has become known as *Reichskristallnacht,* a name that to my way of thinking is almost insulting. So much more was broken that night than crystal! Jews were killed, families were separated, businesses were destroyed and looted, windows were smashed, holy places were blown up, and all our lives were changed forever.

After several days, the terror abated, but even tighter restrictions were placed on Jews. My father came back after a week. There had been several visits by the police, but father had a good friend from his army days at the local police station, and this man finally stopped further visits by his colleagues to our home.

I went back to K. Messerschmidt, but he was not there anymore and the bookkeeper told me that the business was closed. She gave me a good reference and told me to look for another job. Where would I find one? At that time, all girls leaving school had to work for one year in a household other than that of their parents. A friend of father, who was the director of a Jewish old age home, offered me a job where I could combine office work and household duties in the kitchen of that home. The only drawback was that I had to live in the staff dormitory. However, the girls there were all about my age or a little older and I got used to this kind of life very quickly. The curfew was strict, but we made our own fun. The work was hard, especially the kitchen work under the supervision of Miss Zlata Sperling. "Sperling" in German means "sparrow" in English, and since she weighed at least two hundred pounds, we had something else to laugh about. I learned a great deal from her. She was a fabulous cook and she treated us to Polish specialties on weekends or birthdays. Mr. Adolf Braun, the director, left the paper work and bookkeeping to me, and I was glad about having paid attention to Mr. Messerschmidt and his partner.

Marianne had gotten married to Heinz Joachim, a member of the illegal group, and her wedding was one of the few joyous events during those dark times. I still heard regularly from Caroline and Charlotte, as well as from other school friends, but their world by then had become very different from mine.

In earlier years, whenever my parents talked about the year 1939, they always discussed plans for several special events. There would be my Oma's eightieth birthday, then three weeks later my parents' silver wedding anniversary, and in June, there would be my brother Herbert's Bar Mitzvah. My father always added jokingly, "And our Inge will get engaged that year!"

But now that it had arrived, 1939 was no longer the time to plan such joyful festivities. We were still stricken by the events of *Kristallnacht*. Yet, when Oma's birthday arrived, all the relatives and friends still in Germany came to honor this special lady. Of course, by then many had left and those who had been taken to concentration camps on or shortly after November 9, 1938 had not returned. Three weeks later, at my parents' party, the circle had shrunk even more. Still, we recited poems for them, and my Aunt Dorothea Skodowski sang the "Hochzeits Carmen" wedding song, which had been composed for Bruno and Flora Gerson twenty-five years earlier. Herbert and I bought an elegant lace bedspread for them and there were many other beautiful presents, most of them family heirlooms from those who were leaving Germany and could not take them along. I remember that my mother promised each one that she would take care of these things "until we are all together again."

Herbert's Bar Mitzvah took place in the synagogue on Oranienburger Strasse. Rabbi Martin Salomonski, a friend of my parents, presided. This synagogue was only slightly damaged due to the courageous efforts of a German police officer who got the fire department to come and fight the flames on November 9. The rabbi spoke movingly, and the ever-shrinking family group prayed with him and Herbert, who did his job beautifully. There were tears in many eyes; most of us realized that this would be the last festive event in our family. A dear friend, Mary Kochmann, had made special hand-crocheted dresses for mother, Aunt Dorothea, and me, and I can still see us in those beautiful dresses at the party that my parents had managed to arrange, even though many things were already rationed. Again, poems were recited and I still have the recording of the speech I made for my beloved brother.

When war broke out on September 1, 1939, we hoped that the Allies would make short shrift of Hitler and his hordes. As so often before, we were mistaken and deeply disappointed. The *Blitzkrieg* brought great victories for Hitler. There were stories about atrocities against Polish Jews and some of us felt that we would be next.

My kitchen work at the old age home became more stressful, since rationing was now strictly enforced. Eventually, Jewish ration cards would have the ominous "J" on them.

Otherwise, life in Berlin went on almost as before, except for the black-out at night. People in the neighborhood of the old age home had worried faces. This was a workers' section, and they remembered another war, twenty-five years earlier. Most people though, reading the newspaper reports of jubilant troops marching deeper and deeper into Poland, were happy, and greeted their *Fuehrer* with *"Sieg Heil!"*

Some Jews still managed to leave for exotic destinations such as Shanghai, India, and Australia. My ever-optimistic father, however, said, "This will all pass and we will be there to greet the returning friends and family members at Potsdamer Bahnhof." I have never figured out why he picked Potsdamer Bahnhof out of all the other railroad stations. Who knows?

Those synagogues that were not too badly damaged were filled on Saturdays and holidays, but life for Jews became more and more difficult. I have been asked many times why we did not see what was coming, but the Nazis were shrewd in that respect. These restrictions came slowly, not all at once, and my father always said, "What else can they do to us?" Oh, they could and they did!

In 1940, I transferred to the main office of the Jewish Community. This meant that I could now move back home and had more free time. I took a tearful leave of Mr. Braun, Miss Sperling, and all the friends I had made, but I was really very glad that I could go home again, not just for brief visits, but every night. Times were hard, but the year that I worked in that office was a good one. I was the youngest in the whole building among several hundred employees, and they spoiled me. Many a time I found some candy or an apple or a cookie on my desk . . . very precious gifts in those days of strict rationing. The work was not difficult and having so much more time, I was able to visit my beloved Oma regularly. By that time, they had made her move out of her private room and she now had to share a smaller room with two other ladies, but she never complained. She was truly a wonderful person and loved by everyone who knew her.

I also saw more of Marianne, and through her I met people who shared her views, even though they were not part of the illegal group. We had many serious discussions and great plans for the future.

In April 1941, the head of the office, Mr. Hermann Wadl, told me sadly that I was to report to the Nazi Labor Office. He had been ordered to put five hundred of his employees at the disposal of that office for defense work. Earlier my father and brother had been drafted to do forced labor at Siemens, and now it was my turn. I cried all the way home from the Jewish Community office, but there was no way out.

I was sent to a factory in the center of Berlin, not too far from home, and there I met some of the girls who had been with me at the old age home. One of those girls fascinated me. Her name was Eva Mamlok; she was two years older than I, but she had already lived quite a life. In 1934 she had been arrested for crawling onto the roof of Berlin's largest department store and painting "Down with Hitler!" on it. They let her go after a few days of jail, only because she was not even fourteen years old. A few years later, she was arrested again, this time for laying flowers on the graves of the renowned Communists Karl Liebknecht and Rosa Luxemburg. Eva had a child by a Gentile, but she had told the authorities that the father was a Jew who had emigrated. I had never met anyone like her. She was very beautiful, full of fun, and always singing. She knew the entire *Three-Penny Opera* by heart and sang it while working at the lathe. We had no idea what it was we worked on or what was manufactured at the factory. The German foreman, when asked, told us that we produced "milk can lids." Well, those must have been funny looking cans to be fitted by these lids.

Through Eva I met people who were different—they really tried to do something against the Nazis. They distributed leaflets with anti-Hitler slogans, they tried to sabotage the work they were forced to do in the various factories, and they wrote messages on the walls of houses, messages that were downright dangerous. We did not know each other's names, not even first names, for security reasons.

On June 22, 1941, a bright, lovely Sunday, Eva and I were on our way to a meeting at one of the many lakes around Berlin. We had taken the subway; it was crowded with people trying to escape the hot city for a few hours. Suddenly, Eva poked me in the ribs. "Look at the newspaper," she whispered. The headline said "Russia attacks Germany—War with the Reds!" We never went to our meeting, we were too shaken. Both of us had a feeling of impending doom. Once again, the German armies were victorious, and once again, stories filtered back about atrocities against Jews in the conquered territories. The pessimists among us felt that our fate would not be much different.

In September, the Nazis decreed that all Jews had to wear a large yellow star with the word *Jude* in the middle, firmly affixed to their clothing, on the left side of their chests. Now we were truly marked and open to any kind of assault. Strangely enough, I heard very little of such assaults, and I, personally, did not experience an unfriendly encounter. Many people seemed to be embarrassed and looked away, especially the older ones. Still, it was a shock. It was especially hard for those among us who did not look Jewish, for we could no longer go about unnoticed. Before, we were able to sneak into movie theaters and other public places, and we did so even if we faced arrest when caught. But now we could not even be daring. Jews were no longer permitted to use public transportation, except when going to and from work, meetings of more than three people were forbidden, food could be bought only at certain hours—when nothing was left on the shelves—and we had to be home by eight o'clock, unless we had proof of working late. This curfew was strictly enforced. Furthermore, Jews were no longer permitted to have either radio or telephone, and in that way we were effectively cut off from the rest of the world.

We were quite depressed. At the factory, our German foreman, Joachim, was shocked at what was happening. He was a decent man and brought us an occasional piece of fruit or vegetables from his parents' garden. Eva considered him a good person to maintain contact with our other friends and we gave him some of our books to read, books that were no longer available in libraries. When he said that he liked them and that they were of interest to him, Eva recruited him to be our messenger. Since he could come and go as he pleased and was never searched, we gave him messages and sometimes papers to deliver.

One day, by chance, I met Marianne. She told me that her group—the famous Herbert Baum group—was still active. I did not know how active, but I learned later that they had tried to set fire to an anti-Russian exhibition, had been caught, and had all been executed in 1942, when I was no longer in Berlin.

On September 28, 1941, I was to meet a member of our own group to get some papers, but he did not show up. As we did not go to work on the next day, since the machines were retooled, I went to Eva's house. She lived with her widowed mother, her little girl, and her sister Hilde who was suffering from tuberculosis. When I told Eva that our contact had not shown up the day before, we went to the house where he lived. We met his landlady, and she told us tearfully that he had committed suicide and that the police had been called and had sealed his room. We were stunned; both of us realized that he must have left behind incriminating material.

When I arrived at home, my mother noticed how upset I was. I did not tell her about my illegal activities but just mentioned that a friend of mine had committed suicide. She sat with me all through that night and we talked as we had never talked before, not like mother and daughter, but as friends, as adults . . . could we have had a premonition that this was our last night together, forever?

The next morning I went to visit my dear Oma Bertha and stayed with her for a few hours. When I got home, my father opened the door. His usually ruddy face was ashen and he whispered, *"Gestapo!"* There was a man, in civilian clothes, of medium stature, very ordinary looking, and he held a small stack of books in his hands. When he asked me, "Are these yours?" my father immediately said, "They are mine!" But the man pointed to my name imprinted on the first page of the books, and they were the books that I had loaned to our foreman Joachim. The Gestapo official said that they had been found in his locker. Actually, they were harmless, but the authors were on the forbidden list . . . Emile Zola, Thomas Mann, Lion Feuchtwanger, Heinrich Heine . . . all considered to be enemies of the Third Reich. The man then asked me to come with him to the police station on Alexander Platz.

It was a short walk. I suggested that we should not wait for the trolley, which ran only every forty-five minutes, and so we walked and he chatted with me in a friendly manner. I was convinced that my arrest had something to do with the suicide, but prudently I did not ask any questions. When we got to the police station, we walked under the archway on which it said *"Geheime Staatspolizei."* I had to smile. Just a few weeks earlier, before we had to wear the yellow star, I had been to a movie and had seen a comedy where the hero had ended up at *Gestapo* headquarters and had walked under that same arch. I still had no idea how serious my situation really was. I was to learn very soon.

I was told to sit on a bench in the hallway, and the man who had brought me disappeared behind a door. When I noticed Eva sitting at the other end of the hall, I went over to her, but just then the door opened and a Gestapo man in uniform came out and yelled at us to sit at opposite ends. Then he took Eva with him.

Suddenly I remembered that I still had some leaflets in my handbag. I saw a sign "Toilets" and went in quickly, pulled out the leaflets, tore them into little pieces and flushed them down the toilet. I had done this just in time, for a raspy voice called my name and I was led into an office. The man who had been at my house was sitting on the side, and another man, huge and very angry looking, began to drill me with all sorts of questions about the books. Why had I lent them to Joachim? Why did I try to destroy the morale of the German people? Did I not know that these books were of a depraved nature? Did I not know that they were forbidden? He raved and ranted. I just kept shaking my head, but he went on and on. Then he said, "All three of them up to jail!" The man who had arrested me was surprised. Pointing at me, he asked, "She, too?" "Yes," was the firm answer, "this one too." As we left his office, there was still another girl from our group and then she, Eva, and I were taken upstairs to the women's jail.

The matron, a big, rough woman, made us undress. We were told to take an ice cold shower and were smeared with some grey cream. I was so naive . . . I had no idea what it was for, but I was soon told by others that it was a disinfectant against lice! Each of us was given a tin bowl. Thinking that we were to use it to wash in, I said that it was too small. The matron screamed that it was for food. I thought it was rather comical and laughed aloud. She became wild with rage and yelled that I would not find things funny any longer. How right she was!

Just then the telephone rang. The matron went to answer it. She was quiet for a moment and then turned pale. When another matron came in, she told her that quarantine had been declared for the entire jail. Typhus had broken out and no one, neither prisoners nor guards, would be permitted to leave for at least three weeks. Both matrons were livid with rage. They pushed the three of us very roughly along a long hallway to a cell, opened it, and shoved us in.

It was dark inside. A small blue lamp was high up on the ceiling. The cell contained nine women and the first person I saw was an old friend and member of our group, Lieselotte Rothgiesser, whose husband had been arrested one month earlier, on a trumped-up charge of *Rassenschande*. They claimed he had sexual contact with an Aryan girl. A short while ago, I had been at her house, and now she was here, in this hole. She had been arrested without explanation and her only consolation was the fact that her little girl happened to be at her grandmother's. She introduced us to the other eight women. We were shocked when we found out that most of them had been in jail for a long time. When we told them about the quarantine, they were stunned, and some began to weep.

The cell was meant to hold four people. It contained two double bunk beds, a table, two benches, a toilet right in the middle, and a wash basin. There were some sleeping bags on the floor and we somehow squeezed together for the night. Not that we slept much, thinking of our families and of the terrible situation we were in. At six A.M. we were given some dark liquid and a piece of hard bread by the trustee—how quickly we learned the prison jargon! Then we sat. And sat. We told each other our stories and each one was heartbreaking. All of us were Jewish and none of us was a criminal. Some had traded valuables for food, another one was an alien—her crime was that she was Turkish— and there were some who had no idea why they had been arrested. They thought that neighbors had denounced them for one thing or another, perhaps to just get their apartments for themselves. Some had small children at home and did not know what had become of them and who took care of them. There was no room in the cell to walk around or do exercises, and so we just sat and waited. Noon came. The same trustee brought us some indefinable pap. Then we sat again.

We paid great attention to our personal hygiene, although we had only cold water and no change of underwear or nightclothes. At first, using the toilet in front of everyone was very embarrassing. Even the use of a plywood slat, held in front, did not help much. We got used to it, eventually.

One day, we were herded into the hallway and our cell was disinfected. It smelled awful and when we got back into the cell, we found the window open, in order to air out the room. I stood there, holding on to the bars and looked out at Dirksenstrasse where I had so often walked on my way to school. On the other side of the street were the tracks of the elevated trams, and I saw some trains go by. I could even see the people in the trains! How often had I used that tram without ever looking up at the red brick prison building! Soon afterward, the window was closed and locked again; just a little air vent was left open, very high up, close to the ceiling.

Suddenly I heard someone whistle. I recognized our family whistle, the first six notes of an aria from the opera *Faust*. I climbed up on the window—my cellmates said "like a monkey"—stuck out my hand from the vent, and waved. The whistle got louder, as if to acknowledge the waving. (I found out later that my cousin Erich had been in the train, had seen and recognized me standing at the window, had run to my home and told my family. This was how they found out where I was.) He came back and whistled the familiar six notes and from then on, he came regularly. With the help of my cellmates, who held me up, I was able to catch a glimpse of the whistler. When I saw that it was Erich, I decided to write a note and throw it out the vent. On toilet paper, with a little stump of a pencil, I gave as much information as fit on the paper. I wrote that it was possible to send food and clothes parcels. If the package had no return address, it would be given to me. If an address of the sender was written on it, it would be returned to the sender. Such were the idiotic prison rules! I also asked for a book, Goethe's *Faust*, on which the opera is based. That book went with me to Riga, to Stutthof, and finally to the United States! I still have it.

After Erich had picked up the note, things began to look up for me. I received food packages, which I shared with my cellmates, and I was able to transmit their messages on subsequent notes. The matron could not figure out how those damned Jews were able to get packages into the prison, but she had to give them to us, for that was the law! She knew how to follow orders!

In late October 1941, during the night, one of the trustees whispered to us that all Jews were being deported to the East. We were devastated. But the next day, there was our family whistle once again, and on the next day, and on the day after that, and so we knew that not all Jews had been deported, but we did not know who had. And where was East?

The quarantine did not end as scheduled and the matrons became angrier by the day. Finally, in the second half of November the first woman from our cell was called out, told to bring her things with her, and never came back. From then on, a few more were freed, and once we even saw one of them on Dirksenstrasse, in the company of my whistling mother! So we began to hope.

Then, on December 8, 1941, I was called into the main office. There
I was handed the so-called red paper, the dreaded death sentence that
the trustees had told us about. It seemed unreal to read it. I, Inge Gerson, was hereby sentenced to die . . .

I refused to sign the document! When I said that I had had no trial, I
was told that it had taken place in my absence and as I had not appeared
in court—How could I? There was a strict quarantine—the sentence had
been pronounced, based on the evidence.

When I was still arguing, the telephone rang. The matron answered
it and got very agitated. "America has entered the war!" she announced
and motioned to her colleague to take me back to my cell. I had not
signed the red paper, but nobody seemed to care.

When I came back to my cell, the others wanted to know what had
happened. I said nothing about the death sentence at first but just kept
yelling, "America has entered the war!" We laughed and cried, we were
so sure that now the war would be over soon and we would be free.
The Nazis would disappear and everything would be as it was before.

Then I told them about the death sentence. Eva and Lieselotte realized that they, too, were doomed, since it was the same trial. But there
was one chance, one hope, and I meant to make use of it. I had learned
that one Gestapo official could be bribed. I knew his name, I knew the
details, and I now wrote another note to my parents, telling them about
the impending tragedy as well as about that one hope still left. As soon
as I heard the familiar whistle on the street, I threw my message out of
the air vent.

There were several air raids in the following days, but we were not
allowed to leave our cell to go to the shelter. We did not mind. Christmas came and then New Year's Day and still nothing had happened,
either to me or to the other two girls involved in the case.

Then, on January 8, 1942 we were called out of the cell, told to take
our things, and were led to a police van. We learned that each of us
would be driven to her home, where we had to pack a small knapsack
with warm clothes, since we were to be sent to the *Kalte Heimat,* meaning "cold homeland." But they would not tell us where that cold homeland was. After a few stops at which women who had been in other
cells were left off, I suggested to the guard that things would go faster
if two of us were to go to each home. He agreed. I went with Eva and
asked her mother to call my aunt, who was married to a Gentile and
therefore still had a telephone. She did so after we left. Eva said a
heartbreaking good-bye to her mother and her little girl. Her sister, who

had been ill, had died while we were in jail. Eva had not been allowed to go to the funeral, but she had been told.

When I finally reached my house, there were my father and brother, called home from work, my aunt and uncle, and my mother. Out of hearing of our guard, my mother told me that she had gone to the Gestapo official I had written about. He had asked for triple the usual amount as three girls were involved in the case. She had paid it and we had been "pardoned" to life in a concentration camp in the East. But she did not know where that would be. I embraced my dearest ones for a last time and then was taken to another prison.

On January 13, again in a prison van, we were driven to the Grunewald Station, where hundreds of Jews were milling about, all with suitcases and knapsacks. Some were crying. I saw someone who was fainting, all while several SS men screamed and pushed the people into the railroad cars. The prisoners, however, like myself, with our special armed escort, were loaded onto a cattle car. Unexpectedly, while I was still on the ground, a voice next to me said, "Miss, this suitcase goes into your car!" It was my mother.

I turned to her and she put her finger to her lips, motioning me not to cry out. I had been afraid that my family would volunteer to go with me and when I saw her, I was shocked. When I had seen my family on January 8, I had begged them not to do anything foolish, but to stay in Berlin and take care of Oma Bertha. Mother whispered that they had not volunteered. Since father and Herbert worked in a munitions plant, they would not have been permitted to leave anyway. She had come to bring me the suitcase. We quickly kissed each other for the last time. My darling mother, who had always been pleasingly plump, now wore one of my old dresses, and even that hung on her.

The train started to move. A moan, desperate and intense, went up from all those cars filled with men, women, and children, whose only crime was that they were Jews. They had been turned out of their homes, and now out of the city where they and their families had lived for generations.

While I was busy with my mother, the others had found out that our destination was to be Riga. For the first time in all those miserable days I felt real hope, Riga! That was where Charlotte lived, and she had given such a beautiful description of the city! We would be together again and all would be well! Although I had not heard from her since the outbreak of the war with Russia, I was sure I would see her again.

The train ride was sheer misery. It was bitter cold, there was very little food, and all of us were apprehensive about the East. After three days of discomfort, we arrived at the Skirotava Railroad Station. When the doors opened, we saw SS men with dogs on leashes, and some Jews who wore the Magen David on their backs as well as on their chests. The one who helped me down from the cattle car, whispered to me, "Walk, walk, don't use the bus."

While I had no idea why, I felt I had to do as he said and I told the others, "Girls, we have had no exercise for such a long time, so let's walk." The SS men yelled that the older people and the sick should avail themselves of the bus service; Lieselotte, who was quite frail, felt she could not walk in the snow and in the cold and so she joined the people who preferred to take the buses . . . straight into the nearby forest, never to be seen again. She took my suitcase along, so I should not have to carry it—the suitcase my mother had brought to Grunewald Station, risking her life in the last attempt to make things easier for me.

As we marched, I looked at each street sign, trying to find Gleznotayu Iela, Charlotte's address. In vain. Finally we reached a gate leading to streets with old, dilapidated houses, surrounded by a barbed wire fence. Hungry, cold, and despondent, we entered the hell of the Riga ghetto.

EPILOGUE

In the three years that followed, I often asked myself whether the "pardon" had been worth it. None of the other women survived the rigors of the ghetto and the various concentration camps. I am the only one.

By the time we walked into the dismal ghetto, Lieselotte was dead, killed in the Bikernieku Forest. Eva's sufferings ended in Spilve, where she died in 1943, due to malnutrition, hard labor, and infection brought on by the lack of life's amenities. At least she never found out that her mother and her little girl were killed in Auschwitz.

The only good thing that happened to me in those first terrible days was finding Charlotte. She was one of the two hundred or so Latvian Jewish women who had been spared. All the other women and children, as well as most men, were killed just before we arrived. Our reunion was happy and painful at the same time.

In fact, she and I were together at our last camp, which was administered by the Stutthof concentration camp. When we realized that we had no chance of survival after starting on our death march as the Russians approached, Charlotte and I decided to escape. The last shot the

Lithuanian SS fired at us only grazed my skull, but we made it. After all these unspeakable horrors, after all this inhuman suffering, we were free.

That was in January 1945, exactly three years after my death sentence had been commuted. Now we had to heal, inside and outside, so that we could face what lay ahead. Charlotte's parents were safe in the United States. After many adventures, she joined them. I was not so lucky. My parents and my brother were sent to Auschwitz and were gassed there in November 1942. Only my beloved Oma died in her own bed. Until the end, she asked for news of me.

My Aunt Dorothea, mother's sister, being married to a Gentile, had survived the war in Berlin. It was she who told me the end of my family; it was she who received several letters from me, written while at a labor camp in Riga and sent to her by one of the German engineers. It is a great comfort to me, even now, that through those letters my parents knew that I was alive.

My premonitions, however, had been all too accurate. I felt that I would never see them again and I never did. But they are with me, even in my waking hours, and they help me to be strong and able to face adversity.

I am in close touch with Charlotte and with many other friends I made during those terrible years, and when we meet, we always speak about "the bad old days."

I cherish the memory of all those who touched my life and who did not survive to see freedom. My mother "bought" my life . . . and despite all the suffering, I shall be grateful to her until the end of my days!

EDITOR'S NOTE

Inge Gerson and Eva Mamlok were part of the Berlin group in the Riga ghetto, living on Berliner Strasse, the Latvian Mazu Kalnu Iela, right across from the Viennese.

She found her Great Aunt Flora Opprower there and managed to live with her in the same room. During one of Inge's many absences—she was sent out to work frequently—Aunt Flora and her two elderly brothers were sent to Auschwitz when the ghetto was liquidated on November 2, 1943.

During 1942 and 1943 Inge worked at several firms and at many locations. Many times Eva was with her. When the girls worked for the East Prussian construction firm Wolf and Doering, doing work at the Spilve Airport, the irrepressible Eva managed to get friendly with one of the civilian engineers and got him to send a letter from the girls to Inge's Aunt Dorothea. For a while at least, there was some correspondence between their families and they even received some food packages, all in care of Otto. He was eventually caught doing the same favor for another girl and was sent to the Russian front as punishment. The girl was shot.

Inge Gerson learned how to fix cars and worked at Lenta for a while, but then she volunteered to go to another *Kommando*, which turned out to be much further east, between Lake Peipus and Lake Ilmen on the way to Leningrad, where Jews were used to get rid of mines.

Eventually, Inge ended up at Kaiserwald, where she was reunited with Charlotte. They were sent to the *Heeres Kraftfahr Park,* or HKP and remained together from then on. Eva died at Spilve of a blood infection.

In March 1944, during the inspection of the workforce by none other than the "Eiserne Gustav," *Oberscharfuehrer* Sorge, Inge tried to pick up her little compact that had fallen out of the pocket of her blouse. Gustav saw it, stomped on it, and then struck her hand with his rifle butt, breaking all the bones. Lucky for Inge, the renowned physician Professor Vladimir Mintz was an inmate of HKP, and it took several complicated operations to save the hand and in that way, her life. To this day she has only limited use of the hand.

Inge went through the hell of Stutthof, through labor camps and then, during her death march, she and Charlotte decided to escape. Afterward, in Berlin, Inge met her future husband, like herself a "veteran" of the concentration camps, and they were married in 1946.

She and her husband arrived in the United States in 1949 and she found Charlotte once again. For many years she worked as a secretary for an attorney, but she is now retired and enjoys her daughter and her three grandchildren. Her husband died in 1991 after a long and fruitful life, mourned by all who knew him. Inge took part in the filming of *Riga: A Story of Two Ghettos*, and she does some free-lance editorial work.

When Inge sent me her manuscript, she wrote that she had "abstained from describing too many atrocities because that was still too painful." Then, in typical modesty, she added, "There are so many others who are more able than I am to write about what we suffered."

I do not think so at all!

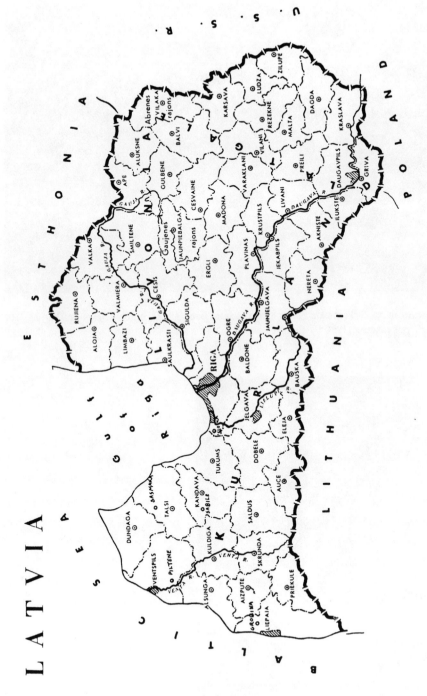

Map of Latvia.

A mass grave in the Bikernieku Forest (Riga) where over 45,000 foreign Jews are buried. The photograph was taken in 1990 by Eric Schneider.

The memorial at Camp Salaspils.

Alexander Levin, 1987, Israel, the author of "The Jewish SS Officer."

Fritz Scherwitz, SS #241935. He joined
the SS on November 1, 1933.

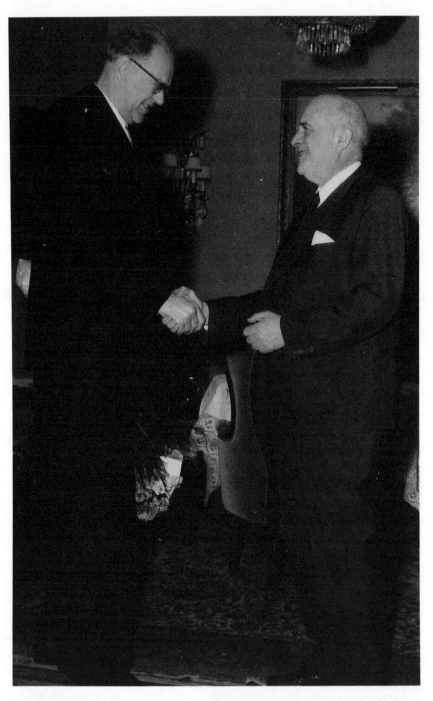

Tage Erlander, left, Prime Minister of Sweden, calling on Hilel Storch in Stockholm on his seventieth birthday in 1972.

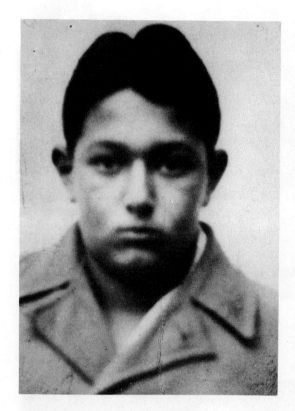

Steven Springfield, the author of "A Life Saved by a Beating," as he looked at the age of 12 in Riga.

Isaak Kleiman, Dobele, 1990, the author of "And the Lord Spoke on My Behalf."

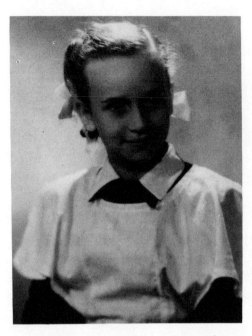

Julia Robinson and her son, Daniel, at the time of their departure from Latvia.

Julia Robinson, the author of "Julia's Story," as a young "pioneer" in Riga.

The monument where Gogol Shul once stood, Riga, 1990.

Gustav Sorge, Kommandant of Dundaga and Spilve, at his trial in 1945.

Nina von Sonnenthal (now Ungar), the author of "The Last Jewish Knight of Vienna," and Harry von Sonnenthal on the day of their wedding, March 28, 1941.

Rita Hirschhorn (now Wassermann), the author of "And I Almost Did Not Make It," July 1949.

Klara Schwab (left) and Charlotte Hirschhorn (right), the two inmates of Camp Sophienwalde who tried to save Kommandant Schultz from the Russians.

Camp Stutthof as it looked shortly after its liberation.

The Krematorium at Stutthof.

The former SS barracks in Sophienwalde, 1990. The present inhabitants of the structure are still kept dry by the original roof constructed by Gertrude Hirschhorn (now Schneider) in the fall of 1944.

Abraham Shpungin, the author of "The Terrors of Dundaga," with Dr. Gertrude Schneider in front of the research center (maintained by Latvian Jews) at Kibbutz Shefayim in Israel, October 1990.

7

And the Lord Spoke on My Behalf

Isaak Kleiman
(Translated from German by Gertrude Schneider)

INTRODUCTION

When I was a child—a long, long time ago—I believed in a just God and I always tried to please Him and my parents. I came from an orthodox family and followed the prescribed rituals to the best of my ability. I was a quiet, serious child and thought a lot about religion, but what was most important to me even then was the so-called Jewish Question. I remember discussing it with my friends at the Ezra Gymnasium in Riga; most of these debates centered on a Jewish homeland and the need for it, but there was also a love for the Jewish religion itself.

Then in 1936 came the sudden death of my father. It was shortly before my Bar Mitzvah to which both he and I, his only son, had been looking forward expectantly. We had been very close and I was devastated. My belief in a just God received its first blow.

My mother and my three older sisters, in an effort to help me, encouraged me to join Betar, a right-wing Zionist group, which advocated armed intervention and struggle to regain the land of Israel. The group had very little patience with Jewish orthodoxy. Once more, my beliefs were shaken.

The subsequent Russian occupation of Latvia, with its freethinking slogans, and finally, the enormity of the Holocaust, seemed ample proof to me that there was no God at all and that religion was just another man-made invention.

A TIME OF TEARS

Riga fell to the Germans on July 1, 1941. The Latvian population, for the most part, was jubilant; not so the Jews. Their martyrdom had just begun. By October 25, after a summer filled with indignities and terror, my family and I had moved into the ghetto. One of my sisters was by then a married lady and I was a proud uncle. Her little boy brought a ray of sunshine into our lives and we needed sunshine, for conditions in the ghetto were awful.

Owing to my earlier membership in Betar, I was part of the ghetto's *Selbstschutz,* an underground organization dedicated to fighting the Germans should the occasion arise. We felt that such a day would come and so, after a fashion, we prepared ourselves to the best of our abilities. Today our feeble efforts seem ludicrous. At the time, however, these plans made us feel more in charge of our fate. All of us were young and totally ignorant of the dangers and ramifications involved in our actions, although some safety measures were taken. For instance, I only knew the names of my immediate group, but none of the others. I was told that this was necessary so that I could not identify others in the event of being caught.

There were five in our group. I remember Aisikowitsch, Isaak Kram, Roma Marianowski, and Chone Rabinowitsch, our group leader. We met in Chone's apartment and were instructed in how to handle a gun, how to take it apart, and how to shoot. Other groups met at different apartments and it was said all of our ghetto police were members of the *Selbstschutz.* In fact, our own Roma Marianowski was a policeman.

On November 27, the ghetto was informed that a large part of its population would be resettled. We were instructed to assemble in front of our houses, and only young men were to remain in Riga. All others would go to another city. We believed what we were told, although we had misgivings.

Obviously, the summer had only been an overture. Now, however, the real tragedy had begun and so, on November 29, approximately fifteen thousand men, women, and children were taken to the Rumbuli Forest and were slain there in a most brutal manner. The remaining women and children, among them my own family, had only a few more days left.

It was my mother who, on December 7, made me go and join the young men in the "small" ghetto. I did go, but I have never forgiven myself for leaving my family on that day—I should have had the strength to stay with them and share their fate. Many men did go with their loved ones, my own brother-in-law included. On December 8, another ten thousand joined their brethren in the forest. Those who had been shot in the ghetto were buried in the old cemetery, which became part of the "large" ghetto peopled by German Jews only two days after our second massacre. The Latvian Jews had been reduced to approximately five thousand, which included two hundred of our women. The rest were men.

ALONE IN THE WORLD

In late January 1942 I left the ghetto. My place of work preferred to have its Jewish workers "on hand," so to speak, at all times. This system was called *Kasernierung* and several firms in Riga used it, since they did not want to lose any more of their workers.

In the ghetto meanwhile, the clandestine meetings continued throughout the summer of 1942. Everyone thought and dreamed of vengeance, but the planned uprising never materialized. In late fall, several members of the *Selbstschutz* opted to leave the ghetto and join the partisans; when stopped by a German patrol, they opened fire. The fact that there were obviously weapons in the ghetto drove the Germans to a frenzy. On October 30, all of our Latvian Jewish police were shot right in the ghetto. Besides Marianowski, I had lost my good friend, Ljolek Genkin, who had been an early member of the Trumpeldor group.

I found out about the tragedy from Chone Rabinowitsch, whose *Kommando* (work detail) passed by every day at our own *Kasernierung* on Gertrudas Iela 28. He felt it was wrong to have let the boys die like that and said that the uprising should have taken place right then and there. In his opinion we were doomed anyway. He and the other men of his work detail told us that in addition to the police, three hundred older Latvian Jews had been taken to the forest and had been murdered there.

We were extremely dejected, although by now we should have been used to the wholesale slaughter. While our living quarters were on Gertrudas Iela, our actual place of work was a large vegetable garden, situated at Rumpmuizas and Stirnu Ielas. Stirnu led right into the Bikernieku Forest and that whole spring and summer of 1942 we were witnesses to the systematic destruction of foreign Jews. Every day we saw the large blue buses bringing these hapless deportees from the Skirotava Railroad Station directly to the forest. The scenario was always the same:

Each bus slowed down on Stirnu and then made a wide turn into the forest; shortly thereafter, we could clearly hear the ra-ta-ta-ta of repeater rifles and later a few single shots. Soon after that, each bus left, only to return again and again. We counted at least fifteen and often as many as twenty-five buses a day just for the Bikernieku Forest. Other *Kommandos* told of such buses, also carrying foreign Jews, going to Salaspils. At times they were seen driving into the Rumbuli Forest, where the Latvian Jews had been murdered.

It seemed to us that our city had become an enormous graveyard, where Germans ruled and where the local population, possessed by a fierce hatred of Jews, was helping in the liquidation and the torture of our people.

We heard that one of the ghetto police, Sajka or Sasha Israelowitsch, had managed to avoid the massacre of October 30, had escaped, and was safely hidden. Eventually in March 1943, he was caught and tortured to such an extent that he told his German and Latvian tormentors all they wanted to know. Sajka had been in the same class as one of my sisters, and I knew him to be a good and honest fellow. I realize that there were those who remained steadfast, and I can only wonder at their strength, but I do not condemn Sajka. Those of us who had the luck not to be in such a situation as being tortured by Gestapo fiends have no right to consider the weak among us as traitors.

In our time it has become fashionable to criticize ghetto police and Jewish foremen as collaborators. This is truly unjust and uncalled for, especially as far as our Riga ghetto is concerned. We looked upon our boys as friends who tried to save lives, ours and theirs.

With Sajka having "cracked," the members of the *Selbstschutz* were in mortal danger, since many of those he had implicated could not withstand torture either and gave out the names of others before they were murdered. Throughout the summer of 1943, the SS went to the numerous outside *Kommandos,* armed with lists of names. Some men on those lists were sent to the central prison (Zentralka), others were shot or hanged immediately. We were kept informed of these events by the *Kommandos* passing us on their way to work. Thus, we found out that our weapons arsenal had been discovered as well. Ominous for me personally was the fact that Chone Rabinowitsch had been apprehended and taken to the central jail.

Suddenly, on the Saturday following this unwelcome news, *Feldwebel* Metzger and *Obergefreiter* Bartel received an order from the ghetto administration, advising them of their Jewish workers' having to return to the ghetto. Four were to leave the very next day, the others a week later.

Both soldiers were agitated. They had gotten used to us in these eighteen months; they had told us about their lives, their families and had asked us questions too. We had done all kinds of work for their unit, and best of all, we had been able to work in the garden to supply them with fresh vegetables. They had known all along that we had nowhere to go and so they had not even put a guard out to watch us, which gave us the illusion of freedom.

There were nine of us: The former owner of a large factory, Samuel Gutkin and his son Max; a Mr. Maisel; the lawyer Max Meyerson; Hirsch Jakobson; Michael Padowitsch; another lawyer, Jakob Swerlow, the former secretary to Mordechai Dubin, head of Latvia's Jewish community; Benno Bermann, a former economics student, and me. Benno had become my very good friend; we shared our food, we talked, and he was the only one who knew about my being a member of the *Selbstschutz*. Thus, he was well aware of the danger still ahead of me, and it was for this reason that he and I had decided some time ago to run away if our *Kommando* were to be abolished. Neither of us relished the thought of going back into the ghetto and, like sitting ducks, waiting until it was our turn to be killed. But we had not imagined that the time for a decision would come that soon. And now Benno was supposed to leave for the ghetto tomorrow, on Sunday.

The soldiers did not make us do any more work that Saturday. They were upset and so were we. Benno asked me, "Are you sure you are going to escape?"

"Yes," I said, "there is no going back for me." I saw that he was not certain anymore and it upset me. "Look here," I said, "if you want to forget about it, it is all right with me. I'll just have to go away by myself." He gave me a long look and walked out of the room without a reply.

Some hours later, when looking for him I could not find him. It was obvious that he had gone, and I knew what I had to do. I went to *Obergefreiter* Bartel and told him that I had forgotten my jacket in the garden. "Go and get it" was his expected answer and with that I left. The garden was only about half a mile away; this part, in other words, was legitimate. After all, I had Bartel's permission. But when I passed the garden and walked on, there was no way back.

ESCAPE AND SALVATION

At first I walked like a prisoner—slowly and with my head lowered; but then I said to myself, "This is not the walk of a free man. . . .

keep your head high. . . . you are not going to the gallows . . . at
least not yet!''

As I reached Moskavas Iela, I saw a column of Jews walking toward
the nearby ghetto. One of them was an acquaintance; our eyes met in a
silent greeting and I continued walking. I went to the house of Mrs.
Viksna, my former nanny. She was a Latvian woman who lived in a
tiny, one-room apartment and she shared the toilet and the sink in the
hall with several other tenants on the same floor.

At first she was very happy to see me. When she realized, however,
that I had nowhere to go back to, she told me that there was no way in
which she could help me. She was shaking with fear and I understood
her, for the Germans punished those who tried to help the Jews.

To make matters worse, as we were still talking about what could be
done, there was a knock at the door and in walked Benno Bermann!
His Latvian friend could not help him either. She lived with a policeman. Now there were two of us! My nanny came up with an idea: Her
neighbors! They were two elderly sisters, very devout Seventh Day Adventists and known to be very decent and fearless.

They were called in and told of our plight, but they, too, had only
one room that they shared with a three-year-old boy, ostensibly a distant
relative. While they permitted us to sleep there that one night, they
made it clear that we had to leave at daybreak.

We left and separated, both of us walking and hiding in parks and
movie theaters, but still we returned late in the evening, despite what
they had said. We were simply desperate and there was no place where
we could have gone. Realizing that our situation was hopeless, Benno
and I obtained poison and carried it in our pockets. In the event of
arrest, which we expected sooner or later, we would take the poison.

We followed our routine for three or four days, separating as soon as
we left the house. It saved me but not my dear friend Benno. While
walking in the city, he was recognized by a German woman attached to
the Military Command, who had seen him at our unit. She called a
policeman and had him arrested. He had no chance to take the poison
and, as I found out much later, he spent a year at the central jail and
was shot shortly before the Germans left Riga. I was told how they had
tortured him and how he had been steadfast. He never disclosed the
address where he had been, nor did he betray me, even though his
tormentors knew that both of us had escaped from the same *Kommando*.
I have never ceased to be grateful to this heroic friend of mine.

For me, that day on the street was like the others before. Late at
night, despite many misgivings, I knocked at Mrs. Viksna's door; I had

still not come up with a solution. The door opened and there stood Katrin Apog, the neighbor. She said, "Thank God, you are here!" and seemed very happy to see me. I was astonished. What had happened?

As is the custom among Seventh Day Adventists, they "speak to God" when in doubt. That morning, after Benno and I had left, the two sisters prayed for guidance and forgiveness. They felt guilty for having let the two of us, doomed as we were, leave their house. They asked God for a sign; then, as Eugenia Apog opened her prayer book, the words on which her eyes fell were "Save those whom they want to murder and do not forsake those whom they intend to strangle." This is the only such saying in the entire Russian Bible, and it comes from our own Jewish *Book of Salomon's Expressions,* the *Sefer Mischlei Schlomo.* It is the eleventh verse of the twenty-fourth chapter, and I was then and am still astonished by the admonition's timeliness.

These two devout sisters took the ancient king's words as a direct command from God, even though it meant great danger for them. If I were found, they would face prison and perhaps a firing squad. As for me, I would be hanged. But that was a foregone conclusion anyway.

Under great stress, in the most awkward of situations, Katrin and Eugenia Apog kept me with them for fourteen months, until the day of liberation. They, the little boy, and I shared one room; we had to make do with rations meant for two, and although we suffered especially in regard to personal hygiene, there was utter peace in that small place, perhaps because they believed so strongly in God's explicit command to them. There were many dangers to overcome during those fourteen months, but these two good souls, with the help of my former nanny, persevered and never lost faith.

When liberation came, it turned out that the little boy, their "distant" relative, was a Jewish child, Joseph Abramson. His mother, a Latvian Jewess, had been shipped to Stutthof from Kaiserwald and had miraculously survived. When she came back and found that the two sisters had managed to save her child, she was probably the happiest person in all of Riga. All of us cried when she embraced the boy. It was a true miracle.

EPILOGUE

It was a very different Riga from the one I used to know. Only a handful of Jews had survived in the city itself. Some came back from Russia, where they had been sent in June 1941.

There were several trials of German SS and their Latvian collaborators, but their deaths by hanging could not make up for the mass graves we found in the forests around Riga. We had known about the killings, but we had not realized how many had actually been murdered. We, the survivors, said Kaddish in the Rumbuli Forest, in the Bikernieku Forest, in Salaspils, at the old cemetery in the ghetto, at the Schmerli cemetery. . . . the whole city was one big graveyard. The same was true of all other cities, towns, and villages where Jews had lived. Nothing remained. Nothing. Despite my own salvation, I still asked, "Where was God?"

I went back to school, got my engineering degree, and joined the Soviet Merchant Marine, where I served until 1950 in an active capacity and later as a civilian employee. Despite my scholastic success, I was still at odds with the world at large.

Among the Jews who had survived and those who had come back were only few from my former life. I could not make new friends, although I tried. Somehow I did not fit in. The same was true with my fellow students, fellow officers, and later, with my co-workers.

It seemed that I felt most comfortable with Seventh Day Adventists, many of whom I met through the Apog sisters. At first I envied them for their belief, but slowly, over a period of almost five years, I, too, began to find God again. It was essentially the same God as the one of my earlier years, yet somehow different. Eventually, a measure of peace came to my tortured soul and I joined the Seventh Day Adventists, without giving up my former religion. After several years I was asked to serve as preacher. This made good sense, for I was well versed in both the Old and the New Testament, and I had studied numerous philosophical tracts, all in my quest to make sense out of the enormous tragedy that struck my people.

I do ask myself from time to time if I did, indeed, become a righteous believer and I think I did. Of course, I realize that I will never be able to fully understand God's ways, but I have come to believe in miracles, not the least of which is my own survival and the years that have been given to me, or the survival of little Joseph Abramson, all because God spoke to the two women who listened to Him and who followed His command.

The miracles of our own technological society encourage me to believe in the miracles that are mentioned in both the Jewish as well as the Christian bibles, and although I am happy that God granted me this additional time on earth and gave me children and grandchildren, it is my hope that I will, after I have left this earth, be once more united with my loved ones who were so cruelly taken from me.

EDITOR'S NOTE

When I visited Isaak Kleiman in late fall of 1990, I was struck by the peace that reigned in his small house, surrounded by a garden where he had just harvested beautiful yellow apples. But there was pain too. His sorrow of not having stayed with his family and shared their fate was genuine and very sad to behold.

He lives in Dobele, a town famous for Janis Lipke who had saved many Jews. The Kleimans had known him.

His nanny, Mrs. Viksna, and Katrin Apog died several years ago. After Katrin's death, the Kleimans took Eugenia Apog to Dobele, where she died in May 1990 at the age of eighty-four. Mrs. Kleiman, a retired nurse, was able to make her comfortable.

The Kleimans have two children; the daughter is a teacher and the son is a veterinarian; there are five grandchildren. When I congratulated Mr. Kleiman, he said that he had indeed been fortunate, but it was obvious that he had never been happy. The losses he sustained during the war have made true happiness for him an impossibility. When I told him that this was the case with most survivors, he seemed strangely comforted. Isaak Kleiman or, in Latvian, Izaks Kleimanis, is the prototype of the marginal man, still another victim of the events described so eloquently in his vignette.

8

The Last Jewish Knight of Vienna

Nina Ungar

Times were bad in Vienna that winter of 1940–41 . . . especially for Jews. But I was young, I was in love, and he was everything I had ever dreamed of. He was twelve years older than I was, very educated, could speak eight languages, and even had an inherited title. It sounded good . . . Harry, Ritter von Sonnenthal . . .

His grandfather Adolph had been ennobled by Emperor Francis Joseph of Austria in 1876. Although of humble birth, Adolph was the most beloved and certainly the most talented actor at Vienna's famous Burgtheater. Earlier, when he was given to understand that he could get an even higher title were he to give up his religion, Adolph used the poet Heinrich Heine's words and said, "I was born a Jew and I will die as a Jew." Thus, he was made a knight instead of a count. At his death, his title went to his only son and when Harry's father died, he inherited it. And now I would be known as Nina, Freiin von Sonnenthal, for his mother and my parents had happily given their permission for us to wed.

Harry's mother was a tiny, delicate woman with a big heart and a wonderful personality. Alas, she did not live to see us married. She contracted the flu and died a few weeks before the date we had set and therefore it was a rather subdued wedding at the last temple still in service on Vienna's Seitenstettengasse. The Nazis had not been able to destroy it as they had all the other synagogues in November 1938, since it was wedged in between two houses.

On March 28, 1941, Harry, Ritter von Sonnenthal and I were married in the presence of a rabbi and my parents. It was a very short ceremony, but we did not mind . . . we had each other.

Our honeymoon lasted only ten short days. We took long walks, we could feel the coming springtime, we tried to blend in so as not to be singled out as Jews, and we talked. There was nothing that he could not explain to me . . . I was very much in love with him and he adored me. We lived with my parents, since his mother's apartment was sealed. Then we had to say good-bye; he went back to his forced labor camp in Traunkirchen, Austria, and I was sent to Magdeburg, Germany, to work on farms. It was very hard labor and we did not see each other for several months.

In late summer the two of us were back in Vienna but just so that we could settle Harry's mother's estate. At first, only I was to go, but I went to Harry's camp and asked the commandant to let him go. He gave him a few days and despite the heartbreak of having to liquidate the estate and handing it all over to the Austrians, once more our being together made up for everything. Every minute counted, but all too soon he had to go back.

I stayed in Vienna. That fall of 1941 was a bad time; the deportations of Viennese Jews to Lodz or as they called it, Litzmannstadt, were in full swing, and people did not know who would be next. Jews were driven from their apartments and there was fear and panic everywhere. My parents were afraid to leave the house; there were occasions when the Nazis picked people off the streets. Visiting friends became a hazard as well. Very often everyone in the apartment was arrested and taken to a collection point—mainly Jewish schools—and then the trains went East. Whenever the doorbell rang, it seemed as if one's heart would stop.

In the middle of January 1942 Harry came home on furlough. Despite the insecurity and the extreme cold, we again experienced great happiness, marred only by the thought of his having to go back to the labor camp on Sunday, February 1.

That morning, while my father was shoveling snow somewhere and mother was in the midst of baking a poppy seed cake for Harry to take along, the doorbell rang. Thinking that my father had come back, I had no premonition, but when I opened the door, I saw the messengers from the Jewish Community Center. We were told to pack our things and get ready. The SS man in charge was *Scharfuehrer* Slavik and I asked him whether we could stay in Vienna, since Harry was expected back in Traunkirchen. He had a good laugh at my naiveté and he, too, told us gruffly to pack our things. My mother was shaking all over; it was impossible to quiet her down. When my father finally came back, he told us that the whole street was blocked off; although he could probably have gotten away, at least for the time being, he never even considered it. He and I packed, and then, with all the other Jews from our street, we were taken to the collection point, the *Sperlschule*.

Hundreds of people were milling around, being registered, trying to find a place. Mattresses were on the floors in all the classrooms, everyone slept surrounded by his luggage, and it was sheer torture if one had to go to the bathroom at night. Those bathrooms were soon overflowing, as were the sinks, and it was a chore to try and keep clean. My mother did not feel well at all, but we hoped that things would get better once we were sent to work in the East.

Friday, February 6, the vans were waiting for us in front of the school, and the Austrians stood there and laughed at our discomfort, at the way our hand luggage was thrown up after us, and they showed how happy they were that the Jews were finally thrown out. I wonder what went through my husband's mind . . . he was the grandson of Vienna's most famous actor, his mother came from the family of the well-known composer Goldmark, he had lived in a small castle all his life, and here this mob was laughing at us! Were these the same Austrians who had adored Sonnenthal, who had copied the way he dressed, who had tried to speak the way he spoke, who had taken off the horses from his carriage and had drawn it themselves? Where was the golden Vienna heart? Harry stood next to me on that van and had tears in his eyes.

We left Aspang *Bahnhof* in late afternoon and after a harrowing trip we arrived at Riga's Skirotava Station on Tuesday, February 10. We were given a choice of walking or taking the buses. It was obvious that mother could never walk the six or seven kilometers to the ghetto and so she took the hand luggage and went by bus . . . never to be seen again. My dear mother and all these others who had thought they would prepare a place for those of us who walked went to the Bikernieku Forest and were shot there. Men, women, and children . . . it was all over for them.

Our own tribulations had just begun. After an endless night in a makeshift house, we three were given a dirty little room on Berliner Strasse, which we had to share with an old man. The street's name was due to the fact that one side of the street belonged to people from Berlin, who had come to the ghetto earlier. On our side lived the Viennese.

Papa and Harry were sent to work at the harbor, while I stayed home with a raging fever. Then, while I was still in bed, both of them were sent to camp Salaspils, a veritable death camp. I truly wanted to die; I felt so lost, and I faced still another problem—I was pregnant. At first I was not going to tell anyone, but after I recuperated from my fever and tried to go downstairs to get my meager rations, I fainted and some kind neighbor called the physician. He asked a few probing questions and told me it would be better if I did not have the baby. I was adamant. Despite everything, I wanted it. The doctor's report landed on *Kommandant* Kurt Krause's desk, and I was called to that monster's office at the *Kommandantur*.

At first, when he heard my name and title, he accused me of having slept with an Aryan; I told him Harry's history and he insisted that I had to have an abortion. "There are enough Jewish brats around and we cannot allow them to live," he said. Thus, on March 25 I was operated on . . . and March 28 would have been my first anniversary! I was told that I would probably never have another child.

After a few days I went to work. Life in the ghetto was very hard and if one was alone, as I was, it was sometimes unbearable. In July my father came back from Salaspils. Very few were that lucky; he did not know what had happened to Harry; he only knew that he had been taken ill shortly after their arrival. We were very sad . . . first mother and now Harry . . .

Father went to work and we settled into a routine. It was easier to have another person to care for, to talk to, and just to be with.

In May 1943, we were sent to the peat bogs of Olaine, about twenty kilometers distance from Riga. By that time, the ghetto had another *Kommandant*, an Austrian, Eduard Roschmann. He used to come and inspect our camp. Once, when he found three eggs on one of the Latvian Jews, he had him shot on the spot.

Although the work was hard, it was good to be away from the ghetto and since it was summer and the hunger was not as great, we were able to gather new strength . . . but not for long.

In November, after a few days in the almost empty ghetto, we were transferred to Kaiserwald, a real concentration camp, where men and women were separated and where our lives were made miserable by former criminals, now our "overseers."

I was in Block 3. My things had been taken from me at the "delousing" procedure. It was very cold already and all I wore was some sort of shift; yet, I reported for work separating metal and would have frozen to death if a kind woman had not loaned me her coat. My father was in a similar predicament and tried to find ways and means to get us out of Kaiserwald. When, after about a week, a possibility arose to go to Spilve, another camp, he volunteered before I had a chance to tell him not do do that, since Spilve was just as bad or perhaps even worse than the main camp. It was too late for regrets and since he was all I had left and I loved him, I, too, volunteered.

After standing in the cold for several hours, we were given some clothes and were taken to our new camp. It really was worse than Kaiserwald . . . at night the rats jumped over our heads, as we tried to sleep, weakened by the murderous work of building an enormous airport and the lack of food. It was the worst winter for us yet, and it took its toll. Both of us were ill and both of us tried to go on despite it, for we knew well that only work could save us from total disaster.

On the morning of April 23, during roll call, some numbers were called, among them that of my father. In a panic, I ran to the *Kommandant* and asked to be permitted to go with my father to Kaiserwald. "Why?" he said. "Your father is not going to Kaiserwald. We are sending him to a sanatorium, where they will spoil him and take good care of him!" Then I knew everything. I embraced my dear father for the last time and cried on his shoulder, but someone tore me away from him and I had to leave for work.

When I returned that evening, he was gone and so were many others, including all the children. It is impossible to describe the despair and the heartache we experienced.

After being transferred to yet another camp, where we built a new airport, we were sent to the ghetto of Šiauliai in Lithuania. Drenched by torrential rains, we arrived there and after a few days on cattle cars were sent to the concentration camp Stutthof. We quickly learned that this camp was equipped with a gas chamber and thus it was seen as a miracle when some of us were chosen to go to work. There were various *Kommandos* and the work consisted mainly of building trenches and roads. As long as the warm weather lasted, it was not so bad, although there was the ever-present hunger and the brutality of our guards. When the cold weather came, however, it brought extreme discomfort and sickness. The old and weak were selected, their shoes were taken away and given to those who were to remain, until they, too, would be unable to work any longer.

Snow fell, and the ground became too hard for building ditches. No matter; we were given special hammers and had to separate the frozen pieces of earth. Once, when I was passing the hammer to my partner— two women shared one hammer—the guard accused me of "sabotage" and made me take off my coat. In my thin striped dress I had to work for the next three hours and then he beat me on my legs, which were anyway black and blue from the frost. I bit my lip and did not cry out. Finally he let me go. It was Christmas Eve 1944.

On January 19, after yet another selection, we started on our so-called death march. Those who were deemed unfit for walking were murdered, and those who did walk were shot when they could not go any further. We spent the nights in sheds along the way and were told that for any-one trying to escape, ten of us would be shot. Sure enough, the next day when seven women were missing, seventy were taken out and shot. And the march went on and the killing went on, and the sun was shin-ing, and the snow was melting, and our suffering went on and on and on.

For a few days we were allowed to rest in an abandoned grain depot; I found some straw and made myself a pair of straw shoes. They were soft and warm but fell apart as soon as we started walking again. After several kilometers of walking barefoot, I could no longer put one foot in front of another. As I fell down for the last time, I saw the guard's rifle pointed at me and I heard a shot. The bullet went over my head, but he thought I was dead and left me there, on the side of the road.

A column of Russian prisoners walked by when I recovered from my faint. One of them carried me to a nearby house and the woman there took me in for a while. Eventually, after joining a German field hospital and being treated—I told them I was a Viennese who had been working in Russia—I was liberated by the Russians. The date was March 1, 1945. Even though I faced the probable loss of one hand and both of my feet, I remember being happy when a little ray of sunshine came through the window and touched my face. God had sent me a greeting. I was free.

It turned out that my hand recovered completely and so did my left foot. I only lost three toes on my right foot. However, it took a long time for me to heal, and it was only at the end of 1946 that I returned to Vienna. I did not want to stay in the city and moved out to Unterach am Attersee, where the estate of the Sonnenthals was located. Its name was "The Berghof." I chose the room with a balcony, so that I could see the mountains as soon as I was up. The room also contained a Boesendorfer piano on which the great Johannes Brahms had played. In fact, at the time he occupied that same room.

I made friends, but it was a lonely existence. I filled the days with writing poetry, much of which was published, and I tried to understand the tragedy that had happened.

One day, shortly after New Year's Day 1948, during a lull in the snow, a man came to the door. I opened it and just stood there, staring at him. "Don't you know me anymore?" he said gently, in his deep, resonant voice, and then he embraced me. It was my Harry, my knight in shining armor, but he was changed. The light had gone out of him. He was obviously very weak and very ill, but all that did not concern me just yet. I was so very, very happy. He told me that he had been selected to be murdered in March 1942 while in Salaspils. They left him for dead in a rather shallow grave with many others. At night, despite the wound on his head, he fled eastward and joined up with Russian partisans, also trying to get further east. He never told them that he was a Jew. His command of their language enabled him to be fully accepted as one of theirs and together they roamed the eastern part of Latvia until the war ended. He got himself a Soviet identity card and went to Riga, trying to find me. When he was told by some survivors that all the German Jews had been sent to Stutthof, he despaired at first, but then decided to go west.

It was a long journey and he suffered a lot, but the thought of finding me kept him going. At the Jewish Community Office in Vienna they told him where I was and he finally came to the Attersee. We had so many plans, but we had very little time. In May 1948, I told him that I was pregnant and his happiness was complete. But he was never to see his son, for he died of a heart attack only two months later.

Our son Harry, named after his father, was born on November 27, 1948. I sold the Sonnenthal estate for peanuts and took my baby to the United States. I wanted the last of the Sonnenthals to grow up in a free country.

EDITOR'S NOTE

To me Nina will always be a great lady, a true "von Sonnenthal." All of us in the Vienna group in the ghetto admired the way she stood up to Krause. The Jewish policemen on duty could not help but have respect for how this tiny, young woman, in reality a girl, pulled herself up and told him, "My husband is Harry, Ritter von Sonnenthal, and he is indeed a Jew!"

She suffered grievously, both during and after the war, but in addition to her oldest son, that last von Sonnenthal, she had one more son and a daughter by her subsequent husband. In order to equalize matters, her husband adopted the oldest boy and so the von Sonnenthals are extinct.

After an interesting life, Nina has married again. She lives in California and both she and her husband travel, enjoy their children and grandchildren, and are happy to be together in their "golden" years.

As for Vienna, in that city of great traditions, many remember the great actor Adolph, Ritter von Sonnenthal, and they occasionally even write about him and how there was never anyone like him. But curiously, they never write about what they did to his grandson. He was just another Jew. . . .

9

A Life Saved by a Beating

Steven Springfield

The episode I am about to relate here happened forty-seven years ago. Yet, I can still feel the pain I endured, I can still taste the sheer terror, and I am still in awe of the fact as to how much a person can endure. I am also grateful to a quick-thinking fellow Jew who, by aping the methods of our oppressors, managed to save my life.

Spring 1943 . . . little by little, the Riga ghetto was being emptied. People were sent to various places of work as well as to the recently opened concentration camp Kaiserwald. We, the Latvian Jews who lived in the so-called small ghetto, were especially vulnerable, since we were a society of men. The large "German" ghetto consisted of entire families, and the authorities gave them a little bit more time.

Although my father and brother were able to remain in the ghetto a while longer, I was sent to Kaiserwald quite early and from there, luckily, I was sent to the *Truppen Wirtschafts Lager der Waffen SS* (TWL), a supply depot for the SS. While life was hard, it was much better than at Kaiserwald. Conditions there were dismal and when I found out that my father and brother had arrived there, I felt sure that they would suffer grievously without outside help. I therefore did everything possible to establish contact with them in order to be able to help them in any way I could.

Our work detail did have a physician, but there was no dentist. Thus, if one had trouble with a tooth, he or she had to go to the main camp, which, incidentally, was within walking distance.

Every few weeks, those people who had complained of a toothache were taken to the main camp and their teeth were pulled—any other treatment being forbidden. I felt that a tooth was not such a high price to pay for seeing my father and my brother and so I signed up. After several days, I was told that a group of us would go to Kaiserwald that afternoon.

In the morning, while working at the supply depot, I was packing up socks. Thinking that my father and brother were probably in great need of socks, I took two pairs and hid them in my pants. I reasoned to myself that they could always barter these socks, if they were lucky enough to have their own.

While standing and waiting to begin our march, I was teased by the other men about sacrificing a tooth. I had told them that I had no pain at all; I also told them that I had taken the socks. All of us were on good terms and I had no reason to be secretive—or so I thought.

Then, just as we started to exit, we were stopped. To my horror, the armed guard at the gate told us that we would be searched. I was terrified. I knew that if they found the socks on me, it would mean my end. Noticing a Latvian guard on the other side of the fence, I inched toward him and, in Latvian, I whispered, "I have some socks; please take them from me and keep them!" He took them and I breathed a sigh of relief. Still elated about this narrow escape, I turned toward my group. To my utter amazement, mixed with despair, I noticed some socks on the ground. Someone else must have carried them and had now thrown them away, fearing the consequences just as I had. As I was still standing there, one of the Germans noticed the socks and bellowed, "Who dropped those socks?"

Since I had gotten rid of mine, I saw no reason to step forward and take the blame. The men in my group, however, looked askance at me, since they assumed that I had thrown the socks away and was now too cowardly to confess. Fearing that all of them would suffer if the culprit was not found, they started pressuring me to admit my guilt; in retrospect, I remember that *all* of them remonstrated with me, which means that even the real culprit did so. I never found out who he was, but, owing to their pressure, I stepped forward and "confessed" that the socks had been dropped by me.

I was "arrested" immediately, taken back to the inside of our camp, beaten and kicked into unconsciousness, and thrown into a windowless bunker reserved for prisoners awaiting execution for similar crimes.

I believe several hours passed before I regained consciousness. At first I was totally disoriented and the darkness did not help. I was aching all over, my face was sticky with blood, and I was not sure of where I was or who I was or even if I was still alive. Slowly I began to realize the seriousness of the situation. It was hopeless. It was clear that I was slated for execution—people had been killed for less, especially at the Truppen Wirtschafts Lager.

"My God," I asked, "is this how everything is going to end? I am only twenty years old. . . . I haven't even lived yet!"

Almost like a movie, these twenty years started flashing through my mind:

. . . How I was raised in beautiful prewar Riga by loving and caring parents, surrounded by a large extended family of grandparents, aunts, and cousins, of whom to the best of my knowledge only my father and brother were still alive.

. . . How my parents worked hard at building up a sizeable business, which enabled them to provide a good life and the very best education for their children.

. . . How during my school years I became an ardent Zionist and joined a Zionist student organization called *Schülerkreis,* where my friends and I dreamed of going to Palestine one day to work on a kibbutz and build a Jewish homeland.

. . . How every summer my dear parents rented a summer house at Riga's Jurmala—the beach of Riga—where my brother and I had a great time sunbathing, swimming, or just socializing with our many good friends. It was truly a wonderful life; the years of our growing up were filled with productive activities; there were cultural events, and it was a time filled with hopes, dreams, and aspirations.

. . . How the Latvian Jewish community pulsated with vitality. There was a network of educational institutions from kindergarten to seats of higher learning; there were yeshivot guaranteeing the continuation of a vibrant Jewish life with philanthropic institutions, a splendid Jewish press, libraries, publishing houses, Jewish theaters and museums, and of course, beautiful synagogues—and all that despite the pervasive anti-Semitism endemic to Latvia and all of Eastern Europe.

. . . How our lives changed dramatically with the Soviet Union's forces' arrival and occupation of Latvia in 1940! Immediately, there was a total suppression of any national Jewish culture and identity. The Jewish theater, the Hebrew schools, and all Zionist activities were prohibited. On a different level, all financial, private enterprise was nationalized.

. . . How a government party official entered my father's business, demanded the keys, and informed my father that as of this moment the store belonged to the State.

. . . How my father, after many years of hard work, having succeeded in establishing his own business, was compelled to seek employment as a laborer in a lumber mill.

. . . How I, with just one more year until graduation from the prestigious Hebrew Gymnasium, had to transfer to the vastly inferior government school.

. . . How our Zionist activities came to a complete standstill; all organizations were outlawed and we were faced with arrest.

. . . How thousands of affluent Jewish families were uprooted from their homes and shipped in freight cars to the vast reaches of Siberia, their only crime being "capitalists."

. . . How an atmosphere of distrust and uneasiness started to prevail among friends, neighbors and families. Suddenly, we were unsure of whom we could trust; it was a question of who was a friend or who was an informer for the KGB.

. . . How the Jewish community, understandably, was totally preoccupied with the drastic changes under the Soviet regime, so much so that rumors about a possible Soviet-German confrontation were not taken seriously.

. . . How on June 22, 1941, Germany declared war on the Soviet Union and took the Red Army totally by surprise, demoralizing the Soviets by its rapid advance and forcing their retreat on all fronts.

. . . How the city of Riga, in the days between the start of war and the Germans' entry, was in a state of total chaos and how there was nothing in the way of transportation to flee if one wanted to do so. All of it was taken up by the retreating Russian army and their administrative personnel. My father felt that under the circumstances, it would be wiser to stay; he believed that while we would be subjected to temporary hardship under German occupation, eventually sanity and the spirit of humanity would prevail, enabling us to go on with our lives. Although we had heard about the Germans' anti-Jewish policies from German and Austrian Jews who had fled and had found a haven in Riga, we could not really imagine that the plans for a "final solution" were already being carried out with the aim of physically eliminating the whole of European Jewry.

. . . How on July 1, 1941, when the Germans entered Riga, they were greeted with enormous enthusiasm by the great majority of Latvians, who wasted little time in turning against their Jewish neighbors with a brutality unmatched by any other European country. They had forgotten that we had been living in their midst for hundreds of years and had helped them, with all our strength and knowledge, to achieve independence once World War I was over. Jews were dragged from their homes, ridiculed, beaten, and, in too many instances, ruthlessly murdered. Very quickly, the central prison of Riga was filled with Jews, and the most horrible stories began to circulate of how the men were being tortured, of how women were being raped, and of how thousands of Jews were killed by the local populace long before the Germans actually ordered this policy. That entire summer of 1941, the Latvians killed whole Jewish congregations, making many small towns *judenrein,* that is, "cleansed of Jews." The Latvian hordes searched for those of their intended victims who had found hiding places and with great pleasure dragged them out of cellars, attics, wells, and forests.

. . . How all our synagogues in Riga, with the exception of one, were burned to the ground, some with Jews inside praying to their God . . . in vain . . . with their screams echoing in the ears of local bystanders, none of whom lifted a finger in our behalf. Not one person voiced a protest, and it seemed as if that whole country had turned into mad dogs, bent on plundering, raping, burning, and murdering innocent people. It was a time when light gave way to utter darkness, when common decency gave way to the basest instincts.

. . . How my immediate family was fortunate to escape this first wave of terror, thanks to our loyal and devoted Lithuanian housekeeper. At great risk to herself, she took to the streets each day, shopping for food and other necessities, thus enabling our family to survive these most difficult times. Little did we realize that the worst was yet to come.

. . . How on July 28 all Jews were ordered to affix the yellow Magen David, one on the front and one on the back, so that we could be seen as outcasts and chased into the gutter, spat upon, and humiliated, as well as prohibited from entering public places.

. . . How in October all Riga Jews were ordered to leave their homes and move into the Moscow suburb, which was to become a ghetto peopled by over 30,000 Jews in an area that had housed a scant 4,000 working class Russians and Latvians in dilapidated shanties. Each of our families had to leave everything behind, being permitted to take only what we could fit on a small, handdrawn cart.

. . . How, after moving into the ghetto, the four of us had to share a small room with another family. Fenced in by barbed wire, we were cut off from the rest of the world. While well-trained Gestapo murderers assumed control of the ghetto, the actual task of guarding it was entrusted to uniformed Latvian volunteers. Bread was rationed: 100 grams per day. Slave labor was instituted; each day, columns of Jews marched out to work for their tormentors in every capacity. My brother and I were selected to work for the *Befehlshaber der Ordnungspolizei*—a German police unit—where we performed menial chores. Mother did housework for some German police officers, which included kitchen duties and enabled her to bring some badly needed food into the ghetto each evening. My father, who limped slightly as a result of scarlet fever in his youth, stayed behind and attended to the daily household chores in the ghetto. We thought we could cope, despite the cruel guards, despite the hard work, despite being cramped for space, but, alas, this teeming ghetto lasted only thirty-seven days.

. . . How on November 27 an announcement was made, notifying all of us that the inhabitants of the ghetto were to be resettled. While the ghetto population was fearful and apprehensive, no one could actually envision what the words really meant. Specific streets were to be evacuated first and the "resettlement," turning bloody in no time, actually was carried out on November 29, by detachments of drunken Latvian and German guards, who administered merciless beatings and behaved with unparalleled brutality. Babies were torn from their mother's arms, thrown into the air and used for target practice, or slammed against the posts of houses so that their skulls split open. People were ordered to dress quickly and form into columns.

. . . How my brother and I, together with about 4,000 able-bodied, younger men were separated from the rest of the ghetto and driven into streets and houses, later to be known as "the small ghetto." My father and my mother remained in the large ghetto.

. . . How I watched the columns, being chased and flogged by the guards, trudge in the direction of the Rumbuli Forest; "faster, faster," I heard them shout and I watched helplessly as a woman, carrying a small child, stumbled and the child fell out of her arms. As she bent down to pick up the child, one Latvian guard came over, grabbed the child by its legs and held it up. The woman, crying bitterly, pleaded for mercy, but the guard removed his gun from the holster and shot the little child in the head. When the mother screamed hysterically, he dropped the child's lifeless body, turned to her, and in cold blood shot her in the head as well. As the column marched on, cowed and stunned, I raised my head to heaven and murmured, "Dear God— *Habet Mishomayim*

Ure—Deine kinder jogt men—Deine kinder schlogt men—(Your children are hunted and beaten) Look down from Thy heavens—Aren't we Your children? Aren't we God's creatures? Why do You let them do this to us? What turned these people into mass murderers?'' I asked, but I did not receive an answer.

. . . How those who could not walk were being convinced by well-dressed, elegant German officers to board the blue buses that would deliver them to the forest, ever-mindful of their policy to exterminate European Jewry at all costs and in any way possible. It did not matter to them that the veneer of humanity was set back thousands of years.

. . . How on that day alone, as we were to find out much later, 15,000 of our dear people, men, women, and children, were led to mass graves in the Rumbuli Forest, were forced to undress, and were then brutally machine gunned, falling into the graves prepared days earlier by Russian prisoners of war. Many of the victims were mortally wounded but not dead and were then finished off by single shots.

. . . How we, my brother and I, found out later in the day that our parents had survived the massacre due to the fact that they went to hide in the building used by the Jewish leadership of the ghetto. They went back to their room. Then, on December 7, my father came over to us, sent by my mother, to bring us some of the clothes we had left behind.

. . . How the part of the ghetto where we had been assigned to was sealed off so that my father could not return and how on December 8, the operation of November 29 was repeated in a similar fashion with approximately 11,000 victims, among them my beautiful, kindhearted, sweet mother—may her soul rest in peace! The three of us, mourning her, became part of the small ghetto, preoccupied mainly with our daily fight for survival.

. . . How father prevented my brother and me from becoming part of the Latvian Jewish ghetto police created to keep order in the small ghetto. In retrospect, his unwillingness to let us join saved our lives, for all of them were executed when an abortive attempt to rise up against the Germans was discovered. Among the slain were my dear friends Sascha Gurewitz, David Kolmann, Roma Marianowski, Monja Tankel, and Sajka Israelowitsch. May their memory be blessed forever and ever.

As these tragic events flashed through my mind, I was aware of the hopelessness of my situation, and I asked . . . after having endured so much, all those years of heartache, all those years of hardship and debasement, must I lose my precious life in this dark dungeon? For despite the fact that our lives were so dismal, I wanted to live so badly, and I kept hoping for a miracle to occur. Again and again, the thought kept going through my head that it was perhaps a nightmare I was experiencing and that I would wake up from it, and it would be gone.

Suddenly, I heard footsteps approaching, getting louder as they neared the bunker, and as they neared, my terror mounted, for I knew well that my executioners were approaching and I could hear them laughing. Murdering a Jew would just be part of their daily routine, but it was *my* murder they were about to commit, and I would be no more, and what would my father and my brother say, and I did not want to die.

The footsteps ceased, the door was flung open, and there stood the two noncommissioned officers who were feared the most in our camp, *Oberscharfuehrer* Eichfelder and *Oberscharfuehrer* Graf. They were accompanied by our Jewish camp elder, David Kagan. Just as the unholy pair reached for their guns, Kagan flung himself at me, screaming, "*Du Schweinehund,* how dare you steal from the German army—I will teach you a lesson you will never forget!" As the two SS men watched, he threw me to the floor and started beating and kicking me mercilessly. They stared in utter amazement as he produced a club and proceeded in a brutal exhibition of barbarism to beat me to a pulp. I was bleeding profusely and still the beating continued. "God, let me die" was the last thought I remember before everything went black and I drifted into unconsciousness. He kicked me a few times, and then, saying, "He is finished," Kagan and the two Germans left me for dead.

When I awoke several days later, I could not open my eyes; they were encrusted with blood. My whole body was swollen and very, very painful to the touch. I could hardly move. I heard voices though, and when I murmured, "Where am I? What happened?" the answer was a gentle, "You are alive and recuperating in the camp barrack!"

After Kagan and the two SS men had left me for dead, Kagan waited until dark and then sent two of my fellow prisoners with a stretcher to get me out of the bunker before anyone could discover that I was, indeed, still alive. His beating, brutal though it was, had saved my life. A few weeks after this episode, when I was working again, he told me that he had done the only thing possible: He had beaten them at their own game! Kagan was instrumental in getting my father and my brother to be transferred to our *Kommando* from Kaiserwald, and we stayed together until in late fall of 1944 we were separated in Stutthof. But that is another story!

I dedicate this story to my sons Stewart and Charles, since I feel a strong need to leave them a legacy of a family they never knew and a life they never experienced. Sons, always remember that your birth gave meaning to your parents' survival and constituted a victory over those who had sought to destroy our people. Never cease reminding the world what was done to us . . . never forget that the greatest crime of all is indifference to the suffering of others.

I love you both very much and I always will.

EDITOR'S NOTE

Steven Springfield and his brother Peter survived and are living in the United States. Their father was killed in the concentration camp Stutthof.

After retiring from his retail business, Steven and his wife Muriel are extremely involved in Jewish causes in the United States, in his old country, and in Israel. He is the president of the Jewish Survivors of Latvia organization, and it is under his able leadership that scholarships are extended to Baltic achievers in Israel, and that new *Olim,* who come there from the Baltic States, are helped to be integrated into Israel's mainstream.

It was only in 1990 that Steven and his brother, together with their wives, went back to Riga, which Steven and Peter had left in 1944. They said Kaddish at their mother's last resting place, in the Rumbuli Forest. While in Riga, they had occasion to hear the new Jewish Kinnor choir, made up of Jewish children. Steven was able to bring them to the United States for a very successful concert tour.

In the *Latvian Jewish Courier,* a newsletter that appears four times a year and that is edited by me, Steven Springfield writes a column entitled "Letter from the President." Although the items he discusses are of a general nature and concern immediate problems of the organization, there is also a subtle message: Never forget what was done to us. . . . Keep the past alive so that future generations will know how a thriving, vibrant Jewish community in Latvia was almost totally extinguished by both Germans and Latvians.

His story here bears the same message.

10

Tough Luck

"Du hast Pech gehabt!"

Yakob Basner
(Translated from Yiddish by Isaac Leo Kram)

I was born in Riga on December 8, 1927. The family, besides myself, consisted of my father Leiser, my mother Guta, and the twins, Abe and Celia, born in 1934. We lived on 91 Gertrudas Iela. Our house and the two adjacent houses belonged to Mr. Milwitsky. Altogether, there were forty-seven apartments, forty-five of which were occupied by Jews.

My Bar Mitzvah in 1940 was the last *Simcha* in our family. At that time the Soviets were in charge, but that would end after another six months.

Only a few days after the Germans arrived in Riga on July 1, 1941, most of the Jewish males living in the three houses were taken away, all of them to be killed either at the central prison or the Bikernieku Forest. My father, at my mother's urging, hid in the attic and thus escaped that very first carnage.

In the next few weeks, Latvian auxiliary policemen came to the three houses quite frequently. They were guided by our superintendent and his son Yanka. Yanka grew up with us, spoke Yiddish quite well, but like many other Latvians turned out to be a fierce Jew hater. In the late evening hours, we were often "visited" by plundering German soldiers. In this way, during these first weeks of German occupation, I lost my very good friend Jacob Elizofon. He was killed together with his father. I also lost my uncle Gutman Feld. Then, in late summer, from the sixth floor of our building, I suddenly noticed that the Gogol synagogue was burning. I found out later that many Jews were burned inside, and among them my classmate Jacobson with his sister, who had lived across the street from the synagogue.

A few days after the burning of the synagogue, my mother was taken to the basement of the police headquarters, the *prefectur* on Aspasia Boulevard. There she witnessed how drunk Latvian policemen raped and tortured young Jewish girls. She also saw how the policemen ridiculed our landlord Milwitsky, stripping him naked, shoving a Russian militia cap on his head, and making him sing popular Russian songs. My mother was kept at the *prefectur* an entire day and night. After she was released, she worked at several menial forced labor jobs in the city.

Then in October, all Jews received orders to leave their apartments and move into the Moscow suburb, where a ghetto was established. I got a pushcart and transported our meager household belongings to 42 Ludzas Iela. It was crowded, there was hunger, we suffered in many ways, but at least we were together. On November 28, however, my father did not return to the ghetto from his working place in the city. Apparently, the Germans for whom he worked knew what was going to happen to us on the next day and kept the entire *Kommando* in the city. In fact, I never saw my father again, although we kept in touch through others.

On December 1, my mother and the three of us, as well as all the inhabitants of the buildings on Ludzas Iela, were chased out of our apartments. We stood out in the cold and snow all day long in a courtyard at the corner of Ludzas and Daugavpils Ielas. When night fell, we were pushed into nearby buildings and in the morning we were told to go back to our apartments. Apparently, during that first *Aktion* only the Jews from Sadovnika and Katolu Ielas were taken to their deaths.

The next morning orders were given that all able-bodied men were to go to the "little ghetto." When the Latvian policeman at the gate asked me my age, I said with great conviction that I was eighteen. My uncle Chaim Glaser and I shared the apartment on 27 Liksnas Iela with Moshe Ratz and his son Itzchok, Motl Kit, Zalman Basner, and Blum. The work detail in the city to which we were assigned was called *Pulver-turm*.

On December 8, the day I turned fourteen, my mother, my brother and sister, together with thousands of other Jews were taken to their deaths in the Rumbuli Forest. Thus, my birthday was converted into a day of mourning that will remain with me for the rest of my life.

During the next year my father tried his best to get me into his work detail, *Kommando* Lenta, but was unable to do so. I stayed with my uncles and the ghetto gave me a chance to grow up. In the summer of 1943 I was sent to the peat bogs of Skrunda, and from there I was transferred to Kaiserwald, a concentration camp in one of the best sections of Riga.

Whatever I had suffered before paled by comparison. Life there was horrible. Just then, in the early fall of 1943, the camp was in the midst of being enlarged. They had begun building it in the spring. It consisted of a number of barracks, called blocks, each of which had its "block elder," the dreaded master over life and death. I was in Block 3, the newest one. My "elder" was Mikush, a short, broad-shouldered Polish "political" prisoner. Although he had been an officer in the Polish army, he was nothing but a criminal, brutal, sadistic, and always screaming.

We slept on bags filled with straw on bare soil. Early each morning we were chased out of our block and taken to work in the city. When we returned in the evening, we were rushed to do all kinds of chores, especially pushing lorries filled with sand, gravel, and stones. We were "improving" the barracks and the roads between them. Exhausted and beaten by *Kapos,* former criminals, we were finally permitted to enter our blocks and slump down onto our straw bags. We also suffered from hunger. The food in the camp was barely enough to keep us alive. While at work outside the camp, we tried very hard to "organize" a piece of bread, a potato, or anything edible.

I worked for Organization Todt, not too far from Kaiserwald. The name of the work detail leader, called *Kolonnenfuehrer,* was Wilner. Our job was to build barracks and bomb shelters for Polish laborers expected to come later. My uncle Chaim Glaser worked there too, and there was Mr. Yoffe and his son, my good friend Faivke; there was also a Mr. Mishkinsky and there was Mr. Jacobson, the strongest among us. Sometimes we managed to buy or barter for bread, which we tried to bring back to the camp. This was very risky and could result in severe beatings and even death. At the camp the bread could be exchanged for something else. For example, several men worked in a soap factory and brought back marrow fat. It could be spread on bread just like butter and it was tasty. I was very glad to get it, but it almost proved to be my undoing.

After I ate it, being unaccustomed to so much fat, I developed severe abdominal cramps. In the past, I had managed to avoid using the latrines in Kaiserwald by going to the bathroom at work. However, due to those cramps, I had to use the camp's facilities. The latrine was behind Block 1, which was pretty far. It was dark there, it had no doors, no water, and it was filthy. Too disgusted to sit down, I stood up on the latrine boards in a squatting position. Suddenly, a strong floodlight focused on my face and a wild scream almost scared me to death. It was Filsinger, a German professional criminal, the elder of Block 1; he ordered me to go into his block at once. He then called all the men in the block to assemble around the long table that stood in the middle of the barrack, surrounded by bunk beds. He ordered me to take off my pants, bend over, and put my elbows on the table. The lower part of my body was immobilized by boards that ran alongside the table and behind which I had to stick my legs.

Without a word, Filsinger took a long, rubber-coated stick, and started flogging me. I gritted my teeth, determined not to cry out. In my head I counted . . . one, two, three, four . . . after each blow my head jerked to the side. I hoped that my punishment would be no more than five lashes, but my silence infuriated him and it went on, and on, and with every blow the stick came down harder. He screamed at me to do the counting out loud and again I hoped that he would stop at ten. No luck . . . eleven . . . twelve . . . I was in agony . . . thirteen . . . maybe he would stop at fifteen . . . but it was not enough for this tyrant . . . sixteen. . . . I started thinking that twenty lashes would be inevitable . . . and I gathered all my strength not to show my pain, my shame, or my helplessness. Filsinger tried to break me. I did not give in, but my counting became louder. Then, when the twenty-first blow came down on me, I asked myself, "Will I hold out until twenty-five?" My body was on fire . . . but this criminal, sadistic man wanted to show his supremacy over a truculent, sixteen-year-old Jewish boy who did not want to show his pain and defeat to that bastard in whose hands his fate was placed.

I screamed out twenty-five, afraid of losing consciousness. For a moment there was silence. Then a scream from Filsinger, "This is going to happen to each and everyone of you who dares to stand up with his feet on the toilet!" Then, a command to me, "Get dressed and come to my room!"

I pulled my feet out from under the table. Bleeding profusely, I straightened up, put on my pants, and, trying not to show any sign of weakness, I proceeded to go to the room of my tormentor.

He handed me a pail filled with water and a brush and ordered me to go and clean up the latrine. Despite the fear that I might pass out, I trudged to the latrine and cleaned it. When I came back, he asked sternly, "Why did you do it? I spoke to all of you in the block and I told you that I would punish anyone who stepped on the boards!" I answered truthfully that I was not a member of his block but that I had come from Block 3. At that he started to laugh and said, "Well . . . tough luck . . . *du hast Pech gehabt!*"

It took enormous effort to drag myself back to my block, and I told my uncle and my friend Faivke what had happened to me. All night long the two of them put cold compresses on my backside. When morning came, it was still on fire, but I went out with my work detail and Faivke told the civilian foreman about my ordeal. He gave me work that was easy; I had to fasten insulation materials wherever needed. Whenever I had to bend down, the pain was excruciating, and I worried about possible infection. It would have been the end of me, but I was lucky. I recuperated, but to this day I bear the marks of this flogging on my back. Tough Luck!

Life in Kaiserwald was never dull. On day, the *Kommandant, Obersturmbannfuehrer* Albert Sauer, shot and killed a man because he did not use the shovel properly. Another man was thrown into the river on the way back from work at the Spilve Airport. The *Kapo* X (his real name was Xavier Abel, but he called himself X) did not like his face, so he threw him into the ice cold water. When the man tried to swim and hold on to a boat, X kicked away his hands and the man nearly drowned. Eventually, X permitted the man's friends to pull him out, but he developed pneumonia and died a few days later. Another man was killed by X in the bathhouse; he felt that the man had not washed himself with proper care. Another one of the criminals asked X why he had done this and X answered, "It is not my fault that the guy could not endure being kicked!"

One night, in the winter of 1943-44, I was awakened by a big commotion. "What happened? Why is everyone running?" I asked Faivke.

"Don't ask questions" was his reply. "Jump down from your bunk quickly, before you get beaten to a pulp!"

I heard wild screams "Heraus!" . . . "Heraus!" . . . people were running and pushing each other through the narrow door. . . . Block Elder Mikush stood there and swung his rubber truncheon right and left, right and left. One of the block's orderlies, the *Stubendienst* Rotbart, pushed everyone out. Mikush had ordered that every man had to run half naked to the bathhouse and get washed.

It was a frosty night. Only the little lamps above each block shed faint light. Chased and harassed, half asleep, we behaved like robots in order to avoid being beaten. (On days like these, my mother comes to my mind . . . my warm home . . . she wakes me up gently . . . in her sweet voice she tells me it is time to go to school . . . a warm breakfast is waiting for me on the table . . . I wonder . . . are there still children in the world who have mothers? Who live a normal life just like we did only a few short years ago? Does anyone know what is happening here? Does anyone care? And what is to be our end? How much more can a man endure?)

Right then, however, there was little time to think such thoughts and I pulled myself together.

The bathhouse was situated between two blocks. It had a water pipe with many faucets, but there was a crowd and it was hard to get to such a faucet. I was lucky. I got to a faucet and washed myself quickly. I ran back to my block half naked, hoping to get to the inside where it was somewhat warmer and where I would be able to put on my thin prisoner's garb. I noticed that only one door was open and in front of it another crowd. I could not understand why they did not enter; instead, they jumped up and down, rubbing themselves to keep warm. No wonder! Mikush stood in front of that door and examined necks and ears of everyone. Evidently not satisfied, he used his truncheon and sent quite a few back to the bathhouse. I wondered how he could see in the dark . . . of course he could not see, but he just enjoyed the spectacle and his power. To me and to everyone else each minute outside seemed an eternity . . . the cold cut right through our bodies and it seemed that our brains were frozen. Just like the others, I jumped up and down, and I vowed not to give up. I felt that I had to hold out; perhaps I would meet my father again; perhaps a miracle would happen and we would survive; even though I was only sixteen years old, I somehow understood that I was doomed if I lost hope.

As I reached the door, Mikush hit me on the head, and I had to turn back to repeat the same procedure, hoping that I would have better luck the second time around.

Still another unsettling episode occurred in the spring of 1944. We had just returned from a hard day's work, when they made us fall in line, always screaming "*schneller, schneller*" and so, as fast as we possibly could, we formed lines as we had been trained to do and after being counted, they chased us to the outside of the camp. We went through a small gate that led to an open field, only a few meters away from the barbed wire fence. The guards with their rifles and dogs watched us closely. Still running alongside the fence, we came to a spur of the railroad situated just beyond the camp. The Station Sarkandaugava was on the other side.

There was a mountain of gravel, unloaded earlier, the contents of about seven freight cars, and we were expected to move it. As we were standing there, dumbfounded, since there were no shovels or any other tools, they started screaming and beating us, telling us to take off our jackets and use them to carry the gravel. The filling was to be done with our bare hands! Then, when the jacket was full, we had to take it into the camp, always running so that there would not be any wasted time and unloading the gravel at a designated spot.

The dogs stood ready to tear into anyone who staggered under his load, the guards and *Kapos* beat us when we were not fast enough, and it seemed that the mountain of gravel did not get smaller, but the load got heavier, and the distance got longer. The first victim that evening was Simon Wolk. He fell and in a flash the dogs were upon him and tore his flesh. We did not dare to stop; we ran with our load, always fearing that we would share his fate.

Every time I passed the guards and their dogs, I prayed silently, "God, please don't let me fall down, don't let me drop my load, give me strength to overcome this ordeal. . . ."

I figured that the mountain of gravel would have to disappear sometime, and so we ran and we heard the screams of our tormentors and the moans of their victims. Those who fell or faltered were beaten and bloodied and bitten by the dogs. A special work detail came out and carried these unfortunates into the camp hospital, most of them never to be seen again.

Finally, after several hours of this terror, the mountain of gravel had been moved. We were ordered to smooth out the ground, again using our bare hands, and as I did so, I felt that I had overcome yet another torture, that I had survived yet another day in the hell that was Kaiserwald, and that God would help me to withstand whatever was in store for me.

On August 6, 1944, we were put on a boat and taken to K.Z. Stutthof, where we stayed until August 13. Then we were taken to K.Z. Buchenwald and I was sent to the Zeitz Brabag Benzin factory at Reimsdorf.

When the American army came close to Reimsdorf, we were evacuated and we walked across the Czechoslovakian border, until we finally reached the ghetto of Theresienstadt. There, on May 10, 1945, we were liberated.

Many of our group died right after the liberation. I, too, was sick; I had typhoid fever. After recuperating for about a month, which I spent in Prague with Yolla Weinberg, Faivke Yoffe, Poliakov, Perecman, Kalman Aron and a few others, Yolla and I set out to return to Riga. I was sure I would find my father, but to my everlasting sorrow I found out that he was killed only one day before the liberation. He had not been able to keep up on the death march in one of the camps outside Stutthof. Thus, I was the sole survivor of a family of forty.

Wanting to say Kaddish, I went to Petau synagogue, the only synagogue in Riga not destroyed by the Germans. I did not know anyone there. Afterward, I took the trolley car to Kaiserwald and then I stood where so many had suffered so much, and I spoke to myself, for there was no one else to speak to. I said; "Yakob Basner, you are a free man now . . . you are the only survivor of your family . . . you have the sacred duty and responsibility to start a new life . . . once again you have to prove that you are stronger than they were, for they did not reach their goal of wiping out the Jews completely. . . . Yakob . . . you have to prove to the world that we Jews are an eternal people!"

I did make a new life for myself. In Riga, I married my former classmate Dora Taitz. We have two daughters, one named Guta after my mother, and the other Elizabeth, after my father Leiser. Both of them married Jewish men and there are three grandchildren to carry on the traditions of the past.

In 1980 we arrived in this blessed country and we now live in Long Beach, California.

EDITOR'S NOTE

The Basners, their two daughters, and families all live in Long Beach, California.

Almost from the very start, Yakob participated in the Soviet resettlement program. He studied English and was soon invited to speak at temples and Jewish organizations. At the same time, he has been very active in the development of a Yiddish speaking program at the Jewish Community Center in Long Beach, teaching beginning and intermediate classes. In addition, he is in charge of *Haimische Events,* a cultural gathering that meets to enjoy and perpetuate the Yiddish language and culture.

Yakob Basner's commitment to *Yiddishkeit* and his many contributions to the community led to his being a recipient of a *Chai* award for outstanding service. He has also won the Murray I. Gurfein Memorial Prize, given to refugees assisted by HIAS (Hebrew Immigrant Aid Society) who have made noteworthy progress in adjusting to life in the United States.

Yakob Basner has fulfilled his promise. He proved to himself that he is indeed stronger than his enemies; he has contributed to Jewish life; he has borne witness against the unspeakable crimes committed against his people and has thus given validity to his belief that Jews are indeed an eternal people.

11

The Children in Camp Kaiserwald

Galina Raicin Klebanow

The most vivid impression carved into my mind during my four years of German captivity was brought about by children, children with the scared look of a beaten dog, always afraid, always fearful of death lurking around the corner, children who never cried or whimpered, children who never knew about laughter or merriment.

These children, these guiltless martyrs condemned to a cruel death, fought hard for their lives, lives that were to end shortly. They worked together with the adults whenever possible, got up every day at four in the morning, stood for endless hours at roll call, and never cried, never complained as would normal children five to twelve years of age. On the contrary, with unusual stoicism and patience they endured all the tortures and torments invented by the Germans and inflicted on them.

Camp Kaiserwald was located near Riga, the capital of Latvia. The wardens of this concentration camp were professional criminals brought to Latvia from various camps in Germany. They, like us, were dressed in striped jail uniforms, but theirs were carefully pressed and well tailored; they controlled our fate according to their ideas and, frequently, according to their whims. They were professional criminals who took revenge on us for their failed lives. Oddly enough, however, deep in the hearts of these hardened criminals, of these rejects of society who knew nothing sacred and respected nothing, there was often a spark of pity for our poor, martyred children.

Each such criminal had his own little servant, who polished his boots, ran errands, made his bed, cleaned his room. Frequently these little children were given tasks that were not exactly tasks for children, such as carrying love letters or parcels into the female section of the concentration camp. It was obviously much easier for such a little one to get into the female camp: He could always say that he was trying to see his mother or his sister. These expeditions, however, were not always successful. Frequently, the children were caught, red-handed, by the German or Latvian guards who would then beat them up, cruelly and mercilessly, trying to make them confess. But I don't know a single case when any child ever betrayed his patron. The children never admitted anything, and all the criminals knew that, and therefore were very appreciative.

In our concentration camp, by late 1943, we had sixty children from two to twelve years of age. They came from all over Europe, from Prague, Brno, Vienna, Vilno, Kovno, Pskov, and Germany; children from different countries, different social standing, different cultures, speaking different languages, but having in common the strange coincidence of still being alive. Among them there were some whose personality and struggle for life were particularly notable and it is about them that I shall write.

My favorite was a ten-year-old boy from Dvinsk, Abka, an orphan. He was a tiny, delicate boy with enormous, suffering eyes. He was very lively, mature for his age, highly intelligent, and always ready to work. We were great friends and he told me about his life. His father had been a cobbler; he was killed in late summer of 1942, in the Dvinsk ghetto. Abka was eight years old at the time, ill with pneumonia and in the hospital. When he heard shots being fired, he ran to the window and saw an unforgettable scene. In the streets of the ghetto there were corpses and there was total bedlam: People were being chased and beaten with whips, everybody yelled, cried, and ran. Little Abka understood what was going on. He surmised that the SS would soon come to the hospital, so he dressed quickly and ran out into the street. Nobody stopped the little patient. The adults in the hospital were worried about themselves.

On the street, Abka realized with horror that there was really no escape and that he was going to die. He started running. He passed through empty streets, empty courtyards, across fields; he stumbled over corpses and kept on running like crazy. Darkness fell and he saw the first stars in the sky. Silence was everywhere and he was afraid. He stopped for a moment and listened to the regular steps of an SS man marching. He knew that somewhere nearby there had to be barbed wire, which separated the ghetto, where the mass murder had occurred, from the Christian side. He searched carefully and found what he was looking for—a hole in the wire. He crawled through and ran once more. That street was deserted too. Abka ran to his old house, where he had lived before his family and all the other Jews had been transferred to the ghetto.

At the end of his strength, Abka knocked at the door of the house. The superintendent's wife opened the door. She recognized the trembling little boy who had spent his short life there, but she was afraid to let him in. Undecided, she asked him, "Are you alone?" "Yes," he answered, "all the others were killed." Behind her in the room she heard her children cry, the children who had played with Abka.

"Mother, don't chase him away," she heard her nine-year-old son say. This decided Abka's fate. She let him in, closed the door behind him, cleaned him up as best she could, and put him to bed. He was too exhausted and too sick to eat. During the night he became feverish. She did not know what to do. To call a doctor was out of the question. Over the next few days she took care of Abka. After he got well, she asked him to leave.

"You must understand, Abka," she said, "I have children. Everybody is watching me and them. They will give me away and denounce me. I am already being watched because my husband ran away from the Germans."

So on a cold and dark evening Abka left. He was afraid. He stopped for a minute or two, not knowing where to go. Suddenly, he heard an old, familiar whistle. He looked around and saw the superintendent's son. The boy was holding something in his hands.

"Abka," he said, "take this, it's bread, Mother sends it."

Abka took the bread and whispered, "Where shall I go?"

"Go, creep into the cellar, it's warm there. Tomorrow morning I'll come and bring you a blanket."

Abka did what he was told and crept into the cellar. His buddies helped him, brought him food, brought him blankets, and kept their mouths shut. The children were united in one thing—say nothing to the adults.

Three months went by. Not too many know what it means to hide from the Germans. Not too many know what it means to live in terror, knowing that sooner or later they will come, get you, and kill you. It is

difficult for adults but much more so for a child who is already overwhelmed by the terrible experiences he has had. A child needs tender-
ness and love, not fear and terror.

But not all children were able to keep quiet, and not all children were
aware of the danger. One of the boys who lived in that building decided
to talk about this mysterious boy living in the cellar. He talked about
him at home. The boy's father was a policeman, a member of the German SD (security service). He reported what he had heard from his son
to his superiors. The next evening, the German SS surrounded the house
and got Abka. For some reason, he was not shot on the spot but placed
in the Dvinsk jail, where he languished for nine months. After that he
was transported to Kaiserwald, together with the last remnant of Jews
from that city.

He became a prisoner like all the others, much like the adults, wearing a striped uniform. He got up before all the others to polish the boots
of "his" criminal. Then he had to stand at morning roll call, sometimes
wet to the bone, trembling and cold. During the day he worked in the
little workshop where I, too, was working. We became friends. He was
a quiet, humble little boy. He took care of himself, washed his own
linens, and sometimes brought me bread, which he managed to steal
from the German trucks. He became a very adept thief of foodstuffs,
but he stole only from the Germans. Although I was hungry, I once said
to him, "Please, don't steal, you will really become a thief when you
grow up."

"Don't worry," he replied, "I'll never grow up, they will kill me
before."

There was so much bitterness and resignation in these terrible words
that I could not hold back the tears. Sadly, too, there was no way that
I could convince him otherwise because I knew he was right.

Once a terrible rumor spread through the camp: An *Aktion* was scheduled for the next day. *Aktion* meant the mass execution of the weakest
prisoners, among them, of course, the children. I ran to the barbed wire
fence separating the male and the female sections of the camp. I knew
that there was never smoke without a fire. Abka was already waiting for
me at the fence. He was scared, pale, and trembling.

"Abka, you must hide," I whispered to him.

"Yes, I know," answered the boy.

We stood for a while in silence, facing one another. Then the boy
said, "I suppose I shall see Mother over there. I'm sure that she's waiting for me. The only thing I'm sorry about is that they did not kill me
right away. Instead, they tormented and tortured me for such a long

time. And now, I would like to see the end of the war, I would like to know who will win, and what will happen to the Germans.''

"I, too, would like to know," I answered.

After that, we parted. During the night nobody slept. Whispers, weeping, sobbing—desperate mothers clutching their children, pale and emaciated, for the last time. Some mothers tried to whisper some advice. Those poor, unfortunate children!

It was still dark when they drove us out into the courtyard. They lined us up, and after this awful, sleepless night, the Germans began the count. Methodically, systematically, they separated the weak and the old. Some of the children had been hidden; the other children, however, who were standing among the adults, were roughly taken out of their column. The rest of us were told to go to work. In my workshop we were met by some of our male co-workers.

"Well, where is Abka?" I asked.

"He's alive," answered one of them.

Abka managed to get away by hiding in a mattress, into which he was sewn by other inmates. He was lying there, motionless, while the SS went through the barrack. Only very few can understand what courage and nerve it took to go through an experience like this and survive. An hour after the *Aktion,* Abka was taken out of the mattress. He hid in the washroom, and the next day he came to work in the workshop. He was paler than usual and his eyes looked larger and deeper. He looked at me with the saddest expression and said, "It went off, this time." Then he went to work.

Not all the children were affected by camp life in a negative way. Among them were some exceedingly strong natures, superb characters, who continued to live their own lives, according to their own interests, despite the terrible influence of the prison camp. They went their own way, unscathed, untouched by the nefarious effects of their environment.

One of such extraordinary creatures was the nine-year-old Jacob who had been brought to our camp from Vilno. His father and mother as well as his older brother were killed in the Ponar Forest. The boy, left completely alone, was living with neighbors who took care of him until the last remnants of the Vilna Ghetto were brought to Kaiserwald on September 25, 1943.

He was a serious, neat, and clean boy who was liked by the adults and was helped by everybody. He easily found work in our shop. He tried to be inconspicuous, minded his own business, kept "his nose to the grindstone," and did not bother anybody. He was always polite, stayed out of fights and rows, and was completely untouched by the filth and dirt that surrounded him. In our workshop, there was a big, long table around which some of the children of our camp sat and worked. The work that they did was not difficult, but it was very tiring. Even for the adults it was difficult and hard to stick to it from early in the morning until late at night. The children, who were always hungry, tired quickly, yawned, and frequently went to sleep, putting their heads on the table. Jacob, however, was always alert; he worked hard, more than the others, and he also seemed to think more than the others.

"Jacob, what are you thinking about all the time?" he was asked once.

There was a sad expression in his unchildish eyes.

"What I think about . . . I think how to survive."

"How to survive" . . . three little words, but they represented the main thought of everybody in the concentration camp. They represented the prime thought of every inmate during his long years of captivity.

"You must understand," Jacob said, "that I know I am slated to die. I am thinking of how I can outwit that fate."

Jacob's thoughts were typical, his behavior was typical, and even more typical was his struggle for life.

Quite by accident, I became a witness to his surprising, nonchildish awareness, his thoughtful behavior, and his demeanor during the last days of his sad, short life. At a time when no adult dared to resist, when all seemed to be lost, when it was impossible to run away or hide, when all struggle appeared to be useless—Jacob fought. On that day in the spring of 1944, when the weak, the sick, and the children were sorted out from among us, as I was standing there and watching helplessly, somebody behind me kicked me gently in the ribs and whispered, "Look at Jacob."

I looked and saw Jacob. A Latvian SS was beating him on the head because he was trying to sneak away from the doomed column. The guard pushed Jacob in the direction of the other children, but instantly, as the guard looked away for a moment, the boy fell to the ground and crawled toward the rows of adults who were just leaving the camp to go to work. He maneuvered his way between the legs of the marchers; they continued forward without missing a beat.

Now, suddenly, Jacob was marching in step with them. Somehow, the other guards did not notice him. Jacob measured and calculated every movement, watched out and looked everywhere; he managed to make his way forward, to the first row, until he succeeded in marching through the big gate with the inmates, and then, still unnoticed, he ran to our workshop, which was situated just outside together with the administration buildings, and entered it.

A few weeks later, however, when the children from other camps were brought to Kaiserwald and then sent to the forest, Jacob was picked up and on a rainy, ugly morning was placed onto a truck. They did not see him jump over the side and hide underneath, but as the truck left Jacob was discovered once again and was shot on the spot. I wonder—what did the little philosopher think about during the last moments of his life?

One bright Sunday morning, a four-year-old little girl who had an angel's face was shoved into our barrack by the SS woman in charge. The child was very friendly and smiled at everyone around her. We figured out that she had been hidden in the city and had been found. She was immediately taken care of by some good people, who tried to make life in camp as comfortable as possible for her. We all wanted to find out from her where she had originally come from, but it was hard to make sense out of her. Maybe the unusual conditions in the camp were blocking her memory, or maybe she was traumatized by some terrible events; be that as it may, nobody was able to get a sensible answer from her.

A few weeks later, however, someone brought in an old newspaper that had a picture of some policemen standing in a clearing in the forest. The little girl looked at the newspaper and suddenly began to reminisce. Slowly and quite clearly, she told those near her some of the things that had been submerged in her memory. In a typical childish way, the girl began telling her story.

"I know these mean and angry uncles . . . they were in the forest together with us. There were other children too, many children. And there were also their mommies, many, many mommies. And there was snow, a lot of snow. And it was cold. And then they told everyone to get undressed . . . and then they shot at us. These mean and angry uncles shot at us for a long time. Everybody was falling to the ground and many were falling into pits, deep pits. The children were crying, their mommies were begging and shouting, and the uncles were shooting. My mommy picked me up and ran over to one such angry uncle dressed in a green suit. He had a gun. She took his arm and pulled it, and pointed to me and then my mommy fell on her knees and she wept . . . she wept quite a lot. And then there was a loud noise and she fell down and her face was on the ground. I don't remember what happened then . . . when I woke up, my mommy was no longer there, I was in a nice room, and the uncle in the green suit was speaking to a lady and both looked at me. I never saw my mommy again, but I lived with a nice lady, and I helped her sweep the street every morning. I was happy there. But then, another mean uncle, also in a green suit, came and took me and brought me here, to you. The lady cried hard when I left, and she begged the uncle to leave me with her but he said no.''

All of us were spellbound. We listened to the child in total silence. The little girl, without knowing it, described in her own way the routine slaughter of the Jewish people in Latvia. She, too, was killed at the last *Aktion* in Kaiserwald.

I also knew two sisters, aged six and twelve. They were like all the other children in the camp, and their eventual fate was predictable. But their stoicism and courage exceeded even our extremely demanding standards.

I believe they came from Kovno, but I am not sure anymore. Their mother and two little brothers had been killed some time earlier. The father was in the men's camp, the two girls were in the women's camp, but only the older girl was permitted to work in our shop. Her name was Lika. The younger girl helped the assigned women in the block to keep it clean.

Lika was a beautiful girl, even though her face was always sad. Early every morning, just before work began, she always stood at the doors of the workshop and watched the columns of workers who were marched into town. When she recognized her father, she ran toward him—this was strictly forbidden—and hurriedly handed him something: either clean laundry, socks, or some food like potatoes or bread, which she managed to steal somewhere. Then she returned to the workshop and sat silently, staring for a while.

Lika's six-year-old sister fell ill; she was sent to our camp hospital. Lika was very nervous. She knew that the sick were killed periodically by the SS medic Wisner. She began missing work, and when she came, she kept running to the window and looking over to the hospital barrack where her sister was kept. Being older than her sister, Lika was fully aware of the horrible fate that was awaiting the little one. So she decided to save her. Once in the evening, when the lights were down in the camp and in the barracks, and only the moonlight was illuminating the area, Lika managed to creep under the barbed wire fence that was dividing the women's camp from the hospital, opened a window that had not been shut according to a premeditated plan, and helped her sister get out. She brought her into the camp. How she managed to hide her, and where, nobody knew. Several days later, when all the sick had been killed and things quieted down, the sisters appeared in our workshop. Both of them went to the door and impatiently waited for their father to march by. When they saw him, they ran toward him. He managed to embrace them lovingly and to pat their heads and tell them something. But there was a loud yell from the SS sentinel, *"Hau ab!"* (get lost). The SS man hit the father over the head and the two girls on the back, and this ended their meeting.

The girls ran back to the workshop and sat at the worktable. The older girl petted the smaller one on the head and said, "Don't worry, you shall see him tonight when he comes to the fence."

For a while all was well, but then the father was transferred to live and work in another camp, so that the girls remained completely alone. Eventually, at the big *Aktion* in April 1944, both girls were taken to the forest and killed.

By the end of the summer of 1944, there was a noticeable, but unusual, excitement to the camp. All those who were living in the city and working there had been returned to the camp. The front was approaching and the Germans, terrified, were concentrating all the prisoners in one spot. Somewhere, not very far away, bombs were falling, and we heard that. Repeatedly, the silence in the camp was torn by the acute wailing of sirens announcing either the beginning and/or the end of air raids. These sounds, which terrorized normal people, were sweet music to our ears.

During the night nobody slept. The SS men, crazy with fear, armed to the teeth, with hand grenades in their hands, gathered all of us during the nightly air alerts so that if need be they could shoot everybody. They also wanted to make sure that in the event of fires breaking out nobody would run away and be free, or join the partisans.

Only a few children were left in our camp. Among them was Abka, who had managed to avoid extermination. And now, once more, on August 6, 1944, his luck held. Wearing a prisoner's uniform, with a cap pulled down over his face, he stepped among the adults and avoided the scrutiny of the SS men. Thus he sneaked through the last control point, and, as an adult left Kaiserwald for the camp at Stutthof.

At the gate he noticed me and smiled. He waved his hand at me for the last time. I never saw him again. But I have not forgotten him or any of the other children so brutally murdered by the "cultured, intelligent" German people.

Rest in peace, you little martyrs. Rest in peace, you little victims who have suffered so much. May you never be forgotten, you little heroes of that terrible, bloody war against the Jewish people.

Epilogue by Dr. David Klebanow

After Galina's death, when checking through her personal belongings, I found the manuscript, handwritten, and I was astonished, for I had not known of its existence. It is only fitting that it be published at this time. As for the original, still in my possession, it will be donated to the United States Holocaust Museum in Washington, D.C.

EDITOR'S NOTE

Dr. David Klebanow, the man who gave me the manuscript written by his late wife, is the well-remembered and revered physician of Camp Spilve, where he helped the inmates to the best of his ability. He recently retired and with his present wife moved to California, having worked as a gynecologist in New York City for almost forty years. He was kind enough to furnish me with the following information about Galina Klebanow, nee Raicin.

Galina was born in Leningrad in 1916. At the age of five, she came to Riga, together with her family. She went to school in Riga and entered the university there. Her studies were cut short by the arrival of the German army.

Almost by a miracle, Galina was one of the approximately two hundred Latvian Jewesses who survived the two big massacres of the Riga ghetto. She went through Kaiserwald and from there to Stutthof, and in March 1945 she escaped during the death march and was hidden by Polish peasants. After liberation by the Soviet army, Galina returned to Riga for a short time but left for Czechoslovakia, where her brother Jasha and her sister Kira had settled after serving in the Czech army.

In 1948, after the communist takeover of Czechoslovakia, Galina moved to Munich, Germany, where she met and married Dr. David Klebanow that same year; they moved to New York in 1950. They had two sons, Anatole and Andrew.

In 1967, Galina died of a massive heart attack in New York City. She was a sensitive, kind person, as is evident from her vignette, and is mourned by her family and by everyone who had the privilege of knowing her.

12

The Terrors of Dundaga

Abraham Shpungin
(Translated from Yiddish by Isaac Leo Kram)

The labor camp in Dundaga, which started out as three separate entities, was established in the fall of 1943. The first complex contained only men. There were German Jews, Austrian Jews, Czech Jews, Lithuanian Jews, and of course, Latvian Jews. I was one of those. The second complex contained women of the same national makeup. The third complex was established in May of 1944; actually, it consisted of five small camps and contained over five thousand Hungarian Jewesses, who had been brought to Latvia directly from Auschwitz. All of these units at Dundaga were satellite camps of the main camp called Kaiserwald.

Although it was ostensibly a labor camp, the conditions were so bad that it might as well have been called an extermination camp. People died *en masse* and were constantly replaced by transports from Kaiserwald, which came on a weekly basis. The new replacements did not last long either. There was little hope of survival and so I felt compelled to keep a record of what went on there. Here, then, is a description of selected events in the hell of Dundaga.

I. HOW A FATHER LOST HIS LIFE TRYING TO GET A PIECE OF BREAD FOR HIS SON

In my section there was a Jew from Riga by the name of Sheinikson. He had been a dentist before the Germans came to our city. He was considered lucky, for he had his teen-age son with him, having managed to get him through several of the early *Aktions* aimed at the old, the sick, and the children.

Even though the boy was only thirteen, he had to do a man's work. Winter comes early to that northwestern part of Latvia, and the cold, combined with the pangs of hunger and the hard labor of felling tall trees in the forest and erecting buildings, sapped the strength not only of grown men, but especially of one so young. At night the prisoners of Dundaga slept on moist earth in plywood tents. The rations consisted of six ounces of black bread, a bowl of watery soup, and, if lucky, a piece or two of tough, smelly horse meat in the soup.

Sheinikson's heart ached when his son suffered from hunger; he was determined to do something about it, for the boy was the only thing left to him. The rest of the family had been killed in 1941.

One day in the forest, one of the Latvian guards showed some concern for father and son and ignored the father's disappearance. The older Sheinikson ran to a nearby farmhouse to beg for food and although the peasants were terribly afraid to get involved with a Jew, one woman gave him a few potatoes and a loaf of bread. She may just have been good, but at the time, in late 1943, it was clear that the Germans would not win the war, after all. Sheinikson, in his striped prison clothes, went to the highway on the edge of the forest and walked, no, he ran, back to camp. In his happiness about the satchel's contents, he forgot to be cautious. All he could think of was his boy's delight.

Suddenly he was caught in the glare of a car's headlights. Inside were SS officers. They were incredulous. A Jew in prison clothes with a yellow star and without a guard? All alone on the road? Unbelievable! Sheinikson's attempt at an explanation was in vain. They did not believe him when he assured them that he was, indeed, going back to the camp.

"You are telling us Jewish lies!"

"You are trying to escape!"

"You will be turned over to the *Kommandant* of your camp . . . he will surely know what to do with you!"

They spilled the contents of his satchel onto the muddy ground and trampled on the bread and the potatoes. Then they took him to the camp.

At that time, the commandant of Dundaga was *Oberscharfuehrer* Kröschl, an elderly, gray-haired, cruel veteran of several concentration camps, including Sachsenhausen and Buchenwald. He was a true believer in the destiny of the German Reich and hated Jews even more than he hated the Russians.

Kröschl was very pleased with the "good work" of the young SS officers. After all, such an escape attempt did not happen very often, and the occasion called for a party. After he and the visitors had their drinks, the commandant pronounced the verdict, "Thirty lashes and a douche!"

The whole camp stood at attention. It was a special roll call. Everyone knew what had happened only an hour earlier. Everyone also knew that Sheinikson had no intention of escaping. Everyone knew that he would never leave his son. Everyone knew that he only wanted to get a piece of bread for his boy, to "organize" a little food. But everyone was helpless, including the boy, who also stood there, with the others, shivering and desperate.

Most of the people who stood there had suffered much and were hardened . . . they could no longer give in to feelings of pity, sorrow, and compassion. They were worn out with grief. And yet, at this occasion, with its foregone conclusion, there was a collective pain, for everyone knew that after thirty lashes with a wooden utensil reinforced with steel, nobody could live more than three or perhaps four days. They did not realize, however, what the commandant had meant by "douche" even though they realized that he had accumulated many macabre surprises in his long concentration camp career. Kröschl now called for a ladder. He wanted his edict to be carried out immediately. His German punctuality and thoroughness permitted no postponement.

The ladder was placed against a wall, with Sheinikson tied to it, his back exposed. The beating was administered by a Latvian guard. Sheinikson screamed, but only during the first seven or eight lashes. Then he moaned for a while and then he was silent. The guard was getting tired and started to use both hands while swinging the stick up and down, up and down. Kröschl counted . . . "sixteen . . . seventeen . . ." and finally he yelled out "thirty!" Sheinikson was bleeding profusely and was barely conscious. Two guards dragged him to the fence, where they tied him to one of the posts to prevent his slumping to the floor. And now the camp found out what the "douche" was all about: Kröschl, with his own hands, poured several pails of ice-cold water over the limp form of the half-dead Sheinikson.

We were dismissed. Sheinikson, however, was left hanging there, with the rope tied beneath his arm pits. We were given our soup and our bread ration, but it did not go down very well, despite our hunger.

The next morning, as we assembled to go to work in the forest, we saw Sheinikson once more. He was still tied to the fence pole, but he was now a piece of ice, covered with white crystals, somewhat like a statue sculptured by a master and created in God's image . . . a father who went to beg for a piece of bread to feed his hungry son.

I don't know what happened to the boy, but I've never forgotten the open eyes of the martyred father, eyes that seemed to ask, "Why, God, why?"

II. WHEN WE GET BACK, YOU'LL BE SORRY!

I remember two instances at Dundaga when Jewish men escaped from the camp, were caught, savagely beaten, and still remained alive! Later on, the punishment for escape was hanging. But in the fall of 1943, at a time when the camp was being established, it was still possible to survive the punishment, provided one had the stamina.

Two cousins, Schabelstock and Birman, each about sixteen years old at the time, did not return to camp together with their work detail, the "Forest *Kommando*." They hid in the forest, waiting for total darkness in order to escape undetected.

The SS, however, with the help of bloodhounds, found the youngsters, roughed them up, and brought them back to the camp where each of them was given twenty lashes with the infamous wooden stick covered with steel. Yet, in spite of the beating, both recovered; I do not know what their eventual fate was.

Then there was a seventeen year old by the name of Misha Kahn. Before the war, he and his family lived on Avotins Iela in Riga. He knew that his father was at one of the other satellite camps attached to Kaiserwald and he wanted to join him.

Kahn was tall and blond and did not look Jewish at all. Somehow he had managed to obtain civilian clothing—by this time we wore the striped prison "zebra" outfits—and entered a railroad car without a ticket. Soon after his arrival in Riga, he was caught by a Latvian patrol and brought back to Dundaga.

He received the usual treatment . . . perhaps even more of it, since the commandant was quite angry at the youngster's nerve. Yet, Kahn recuperated and in July 1944, when the Dundaga inmates were marched to Libau (Liepaja), he managed to escape on the way, while the column of men walked through the forest.

He joined the partisans and was liberated in May 1945. A few years passed and after realizing that he would not be happy staying in Latvia, he went to Holland as a tourist, where he used his considerable escape talents to absent himself from the other Soviet tourists. He did not return to Russia. I have heard rumors that he is now living in the United States.

III. THE BATHING KOMMANDO

The winter of 1943-44 in Kurland was extremely severe. Most of the time, the temperature hovered at minus twenty-five degrees Celsius, and since our camp had little in the way of amenities, we suffered terribly.

Kommandant Kröschl had a problem: What was he going to do with the corpses? There were many deaths, but since the ground was frozen and hard like a rock, there was no way to bury all those weak Jews who died like flies. Up until November, it had been possible to bury the victims in the sandy soil around the camp by literally hewing out large holes and then covering them up again. The hewing had been difficult and took time, but now, with the temperature so low, it could simply not be done.

Overwhelmed by the pile of bodies, Kröschl had an idea! He considered it a brilliant solution! Since the camp was only twenty kilometers inland from the Baltic Sea, he would, as often as necessary, send a detachment of Jews to the sea, put holes in the ice if needed, and slip in the corpses, one by one. It never occurred to him to consult with anyone about his plan. After all, he was an undisputed ruler, with power over life and death. Thus, during the months of January, February, and March 1944, twice a week, the burial detachment and their cargo made their way to the beach and got rid of the dead.

Then, in April, the ice began to melt. The Latvians who lived near the sea began to find floating bodies. Fishermen caught them in their nets. A great clamor went up, since it was not hard to figure out that the dead were Jews, most of whom had their tattered, striped clothing hanging on their bloated corpses. Kröschl panicked. He did not want to be accused of polluting the sea with typhoid-infested Jews, especially since his fellow Germans were extremely scared of that particular disease. He also rather belatedly realized that the tide could bring these bodies to neutral Sweden, where the International Red Cross had its representatives.

His panic came too late. Only a few days after the first bodies came to the surface, a commission of high-ranking SS officers arrived at Dundaga, and the upshot was that Kröschl was relieved of his post and transferred to another camp.

Kröschl's successor was Gustav Sorge, nicknamed the Iron Gustav. His first task after arrival at the camp was to correct the mistake made by the former commandant in regard to the floating bodies. He selected a special *Kommando* made up for the most part of so-called *Muslims*. In camp jargon that meant people who had lost their strength, their hope, and perhaps even their memories. They usually did not work much anymore either, but lingered on, always hoping to find something, anything at all, to eat.

Sorge had thought of a nice name for this special work detail. He called it the Bathing *Kommando*. Because of its name, there were several men who actually volunteered to be part of it, thinking that they would be assigned to work in a warm bathhouse. To their great disappointment, they wound up in the ice cold waters of the Baltic Sea.

Daily, on open vans, the work detail was taken to the seashore. Once there, the men had to wade into the sea until the water came up to their shoulders, and then they had to pull the bodies that were now coming up in ever greater numbers to the shore. After that, each such corpse was doused with gasoline, put on a pyre, and turned into ashes. While it burned, the men were chased back into the water to try and pull out more of the floating corpses.

The conditions were so bad that every single day at least one member of the work detail joined the corpses and was burned right at the beach in the same way as those he had helped to pull out of the sea.

In this fashion, after several weeks, the Baltic Sea was cleansed of Jewish bodies and the Bathing *Kommando* was not needed anymore.

I am dedicating the foregoing tale to Hermann Goldberg, then a young boy, who hailed from Kuldiga and who, in 1940, moved to Riga, together with his family. His parents, brothers, and sister perished in the Riga ghetto. Only he and his uncle, Harry Goldberg, survived the two big massacres. The two of them ended up in Dundaga, where they lived in the same plywood tent as I did.

Although young Hermann survived the Bathing *Kommando*, he eventually succumbed to typhoid fever and is buried in Dundaga.

IV. THE OLD, INVALID MOTHER

It was January 1944. Wet snow was falling and a cold wind was blowing, coming from the direction of the Baltic Sea. There was a commotion at the gate. All returning work details were to march straight to the Appell Platz, the square where roll call was held. No one was permitted to enter the plywood huts. There was some excitement . . . another Jew working in the forest had escaped.

Suddenly, there was noise; we heard the baying of bloodhounds, and then there came the familiar order *"Muetzen ab!"* meaning that we had to take off our caps, all at the same time. The escapee had been found. His tattered clothes were carried in by two SS men, with the dogs straining against their leashes, still snapping at the material. Two other SS men brought in the bloodied, beaten man and paraded him in front of us. He could hardly walk. I took a closer look . . . oh my God, it was my old friend Fleischmann! He looked at me, just for a second . . .

I remembered what a good son he was to his invalid mother. Both of them had come to Riga from Jelgava (Mitau) in the early thirties, hoping that physicians there would be able to help her.

We were part of the same circle, he and I, although he was a few years older, and I remembered while standing there, in Dundaga, that whenever the gang stayed out late, he would excuse himself, saying that he had to go and take care of his mother. Some of us could not understand his devotion; in fact, we were sometimes annoyed at him when he left in the middle of a dance or a party.

I lost sight of him, but then in early November of 1941 I met him in the ghetto of Riga. I remember how shocked I was at his appearance . . . he had gotten so old! He told me that he had worked on the railroad during the Russian occupation from 1940 to 1941, and I asked him why he did not use his connections to escape from Latvia. Looking at me strangely, he said, "How could I leave my mother?"

Only a few weeks later, it was she who left him . . . she was taken to the Rumbuli Forest and killed in the big *Aktion* of November 29, 1941.

And now, right here in Dundaga, Fleischmann's minutes on this earth were counted.

Kommandant Gustav Sorge, the Iron Gustav, was very correct. With his own hands he took the rope, fashioned a noose, and, using one of the strong tree branches right at the edge of the camp, put the noose around Fleischmann's neck. Sorge had to hold him up, for his victim was exhausted from the beating he got after being found . . . but Sorge was a strong man and the job was soon done. All was quiet once more.

That night and the next morning, Fleischmann's body hung from the tree. In contrast to other victims whom I saw hanged during these last few years, he seemed to be at peace. His face was serene . . . almost as if he wanted to say, "I am better off now; I am reunited with my dear, old invalid mother."

V. THE IRON GUSTAV

Rumor had it that at one time, long after the war was over, Sorge made the following comment about himself, "All SS men were beasts, but I was the worst one!"

His story was a familiar one. Having started out on a criminal career in the late 1920s, he was in jail when the Nazis came to power. Two years later, in 1935, when they needed reliable personnel for the new German concentration camps, which were then holding political prisoners, many of the criminal element in the various jails were recruited and were made into *Kapos*. They were, in fact, overseers of their own countrymen. Sorge was of such a brutal nature that his charges called him *Der Eiserne Gustav*.

His prison term expired in 1938. Although he was permitted to join the ranks of the SS, he could not join the officers' corps because of his criminal past. This embittered him greatly. Having been an "ordinary" SS man, however, proved to be a decided advantage in May 1945. He was taken prisoner by the Russians in East Germany and, at what was called the Sachsenhausen Trial, he received a sentence of twenty-five years hard labor in Siberia. He remained there only until 1956. Due to Khrushchev's new policies, Sorge was returned to East Germany.

Not long after his release, he made his way to West Germany and went back to his "old" profession, breaking into stores and apartments, robbing, stealing, and selling the loot to fences. At one such occasion he was apprehended and during the ensuing trial his true past came to life.

Survivors of Dundaga came and testified. He sat there and listened and it seemed as if he enjoyed hearing his misdeeds. Other survivors, who had suffered under his reign in Spilve, came and told similar tales.

The West German Court sentenced him to eight years, indicating that he had already spent much of the postwar years in Siberia and was therefore punished enough. It is questionable whether the people who died in his Bathing *Kommando*, or Fleischmann, or others who felt his malice, would agree.

VI. THE FIVE HUNGARIAN CAMPS

The conditions at all the Dundaga camps were abysmal, but the worst suffering was experienced by the approximately 5,000 Hungarian girls who had come there directly from Auschwitz in May 1944.

They wore gray prison shifts, they had no underwear or socks, they wore wooden clogs that they kept losing while walking, and their hair was shorn. They were a ghostly sight. Yet, only a few weeks earlier, they had still been at home!

All of them were quite young. The older ones among them had lost their lives in the gas chambers of Auschwitz. In fact, when we questioned them, the girls would point up to the sky, explaining that their loved ones had gone up in smoke! Although we were veterans of ghettos and other camps, up to now gas had not been a part of our vocabulary. We knew all about mass graves, but gas and crematoria? Our minds were unable to comprehend this new horror.

We tried to help the girls, but we had very little ourselves. During the summer months there was at least the warmth, which helped, even though the labor in the forest was hard for them. I can still see them carrying the logs, trying not to slip and fall, and somehow bewildered by their suffering. Many made their long dresses shorter and used the material to fashion underwear. They slept on the earth in their huts and it seemed that the sun never reached those.

We had trouble communicating with them, since most of them spoke only Hungarian or Slovakian. Some knew Romanian too, but all those languages were not part of our knowledge.

By July 1944, when they left on the march to Libau, there were only about three thousand of them left.

VII. THE LAST THREE HUNDRED DAYS

One day in February 1944, as I was standing in line for my ration of watery pea soup, the handsome man next to me started a conversation. He was blond, broad shouldered, and athletic. He looked more like a Latvian than a Jew. His name was Mendel Poliak, he was originally from Riga, and he, too, had lost his entire family during the bloody days of November 29 to December 8, 1941.

After the massacre he had worked for the SS at one of the *Truppen Wirtschafts Lager,* or TWL, located at Mühlgraben. It was a supply center, one of many, for the SS troops stationed in Riga and the vicinity, as well as at other locations in Latvia.

After TWL, Mendel was sent to Kaiserwald and from there to Dundaga. Just that morning, by coincidence, he had met up with one of the low-ranking officers whom he had known at TWL. The officer, Willy Wichmann, recognized Mendel Poliak, remembered him as a good worker, and asked him to form a work detail that would unload freight trains coming in with supplies. Until he met Mendel, Wichmann had used Russian prisoners for this job, but he said he would prefer Jewish prisoners, since he could communicate with them. Mendel was overjoyed and promised to do his best. I was the first one he asked and, needless to say, I volunteered immediately. For me, it was a God-sent opportunity. Just recently I had spent a few days in the infirmary, and I knew that I could not last much longer working in the forest.

Mendel soon had his quota of twenty able-bodied Jews together. We came from all countries and from all walks of life. Wichmann had found five women as well, and the *Kommando* took shape.

While the women cleaned the SS barracks and sorted the supplies, the men unloaded the freight trains. There was furniture from the Carpathian mountains, shoes and boots from Czechoslovakia, tobacco and cigarettes from Bulgaria, macaroons from Italy, meat from Hungary, as well as the finest alcoholic beverages from France. We were stunned by the array of luxurious items, and the unloading often became a guessing game. We worked very hard, since the trains came at odd times and we had to be ready for them, but it was far better than felling trees or building roads. Furthermore, to keep up our strength, *Oberscharfuehrer* Wichmann saw to it that we were well fed. We got as much bread as we could eat, we got a thick soup, and often we had enough to bring some of the food into the camp, where our unfortunate brethren were slowly starving.

Since the arrival of the freight trains was unpredictable and Wichmann tired of having to haul us all the way from the camp to the railroad station, located near the town of Dundaga, he obtained permission from Gustav Sorge to have the twenty-five of us right there, in the center of town. Wichmann sweetened the deal by giving Sorge a case of fine French cognac and one thousand expensive Bulgarian cigarettes.

First, all twenty-five of us were taken to a military bathhouse, where we were given a piece of soap for a good scrub down; we were also given disinfectant and afterward a German medic checked us for lice and shaved off our hair. We looked funny but we were clean. Best of all, we got fairly decent underwear and new, striped prisoner suits. In addition, we were also given Russian soldiers' boots.

We were housed in an apartment right in the center of Dundaga. The women got the small room, and the men used the large room with bunk beds. We were right next to the bakery; they baked only three times a week and mainly for the Latvian population still there. There was also an electric station, but the greater part of the square was taken up by large warehouses of the *Truppen Wirtschafts Lager,* filled up to the rafters with the items from the freight trains.

Wichmann saw to it that we had warm blankets, cooking pots, and eating utensils. We were heavily guarded, as was the entire area, and after work we had to stay in our rooms, except for going to the toilets or to the water well.

Each one of us got his orders at 7:00 every morning from one of the German soldiers. One person in our group, Matis Frost, had a steady "job." He was a tailor; in fact, he was a very good tailor. He came from Riga and was only twenty-six at the time, but he was quite handy with the needle. In addition to his sewing work, he took care of Wichmann's and Major Puchecker's apartment, where he spent most of the day, in a corner of their dining room. So as not to offend any SS officers, Matis wore a civilian suit, given to him by the resourceful Wichmann. Although of relatively low rank, he knew how to provide the officers with various "perks," and in that way he even charmed the Iron Gustav, who seemed to have forgotten about us.

Since our work was so varied, we got to know many Latvians. They were permitted to remain in that section of Latvia only because of their skills. Among them were mechanics, blacksmiths, and railroad workers. Their attitude toward us fluctuated with the proximity of the Russian army. We could always tell when the Russians won a battle—the Latvians behaved in a friendly manner. But we knew even more, since Matis Frost had access to German newspapers and the radio.

Toward the end of June our German personnel became quite nervous. It seemed that the Russian forces were coming toward Kurland from several directions at once, obviously in an effort to encircle this northernmost part of Latvia. In the east, the Russians were not too far away from Riga either, but the fighting changed the picture there almost daily. The German troops were rather superior at that point, but those in Kurland were very young and inexperienced.

They became panicky and started to destroy the goods that were stored in the warehouses, their value notwithstanding. As we were watching this destruction, Matis came back from Wichmann's apartment in a very agitated state. I was the first one he met and as we were alone, in front of our apartment, he told me that in Wichmann's absence, Major Puchecker had just received a phone call from *Kommandant* Gustav Sorge, informing the major that all of us were to be brought back to the main camp within the hour, ostensibly to be evacuated from Latvia to Germany.

Now I became agitated too. The word "evacuation" had an ominous ring to it. How could it be? Here they were destroying essential items for their own sustenance . . . and at the same time they were going to transport Jews? . . . it just did not make sense. Logic decreed that we were to be finished off in the nearby forest.

My gut reaction was to escape! Right then! When I said it to Matis, he agreed. Where would we go?

Adjacent to the warehouses was a rather large house in which several of the Latvian families lived, each in their own apartment. The landlord and owner was a blacksmith, who had a wife and daughter. We knew him well. The other one we knew was a railroad worker, who had a wife and children. He seemed to be a nice man and we always exchanged greetings with him at the railroad yard. As for the other families, we had very little to do with them. One of the large rooms on the main floor of the house was used by the guards who patrolled the area twenty-four hours a day.

Between this house and the warehouse was a large barn in which every one of those Latvian families had a section where they kept a cow, a goat, some pigs, and chickens. The barn had an attic in which each family kept fresh hay, and it was precisely this attic that seemed right for our scheme. It was like hiding in the lion's den, right under the noses of the guards. But first we had to find a way to get in. The main door to the barn was kept locked, but on the back wall of the barn there was an opening, roughly three feet by three feet, used only in the summer to get rid of the various animals' excrement. It was this opening or nothing. Since Matis wore civilian clothes, he was first to go. He waited until the guard on duty passed and then crawled through the hole.

I wore a green overall under my striped suit. Taking off the latter, I waited until the guard had passed by again, then ran to the edge of the forest, dropped the suit and eventually crawled into the barn and up into the attic where Matis had already become worried. He was glad to see me and now both of us buried ourselves in the hay, keeping close to the wall so that we could observe through the cracks what was going on outside.

The first thing we saw or rather heard was Major Puchecker's complaint about Matis having polished one boot only, leaving the other one dirty. He was speaking to Willy Wichmann, who had just returned. After telling him about the dirty boot, Puchecker told him what Sorge had said on the telephone.

Wichmann now called his Jews and told them to line up in front of the house. We watched breathlessly as he realized that he had only twenty-three prisoners instead of twenty-five! As he was still standing there, shaking his head in disbelief, Sorge arrived with a detachment of SS men to pick up the Jews and presumably, some more sustenance for himself.

We saw them searching the area. Bloodhounds were brought. Almost immediately they found the striped suit in the forest and from what they were saying it was clear that they had no more time to actually comb the forest for the escapees. It was time for them to leave, since they were to meet up with columns coming from other nearby camps. Matis and I were not only glad that they were in a rush, but also that they did not execute others for our having run away, as was done in such cases. Both of us were relieved and when everything quieted down, we fell asleep.

The way we had imagined our future was to stay in the attic two or even three days, and then make our way to the Russian front. By morning, however, we realized that we had a dilemma on our hands . . . the place was swarming with German soldiers! They continued coming all day and there were hundreds of trucks, motorcycles, and tanks all around us.

They were quite different from the soldiers we had dealt with up to now. It was evident that they were frontline fighters, and it soon became clear that they intended to stay in Dundaga, since they began to settle down in the warehouses and other, empty buildings. From their conversation, which we could clearly hear, we soon figured out that they had broken through the Russian lines near Jelgava and had now regrouped to fight in order to hold Kurland. They dug trenches and foxholes, they started to mount equipment, such as anti-aircraft guns, and they seemed in good spirits. Among them were soldiers who spoke Russian, obviously members of the renegade Vlasov army assigned to artillery units.

Leaving our hiding place under those circumstances was out of the question, and we became rather nervous. Matis shared his last piece of bread with me, but by the third night we were suffering. It was the thirst that was so hard to take, not just the hunger. There were some cooked potatoes next to the pigs, together with a bowl of water and it took no time for us to finish both.

By the fifth day, when hunger and thirst became unbearable, I decided to climb down from the hay in the attic and wait for the blacksmith's wife, Mrs. Mathilde Makevich. She had to come and milk the cow as well as feed her other animals. I rationalized that she would not say "no" to my pleas for help, owing to the fact that the Russians were not that far away. I also knew that she was a pious Lutheran and so, as she started milking, I called out to her in Latvian, "If you trust in God, you will not turn us in. Please bring us some water!" Mrs. Makevich almost fainted. She got up, mumbled something, and left the barn. Matis had climbed down too and we looked at each other. In the next few minutes our fate would be decided. . . .

We were lucky. She returned with a full pail of water, which we gulped down. Then she told us that she would have to confide in one of the neighbors, since she, herself, was unable to help us. We were afraid, but she was adamant. Several hours later, a plainly dressed woman came into the barn and called out, "Boys, where are you? Come down— don't be afraid!"

We came and she told us that her name was Klara Vanags, and we remembered seeing her before. She promised to share her food with us and before she left she said, "The Russians will soon be here!"

From then on, it was she who came to milk the Makevich cow. The pail she used had a double bottom and she always managed to put some bread into it. She also left us a bottle of milk. Our lives depended on her, since Mrs. Makevich, the owner of the house, came to the barn very rarely. Eventually, Mrs. Vanags introduced us to her husband Anton and her daughter Skaidrite, age sixteen. They were plain people— he was just a common laborer who shoveled coal at the railroad station—but they were good people.

July, August, and September passed by quickly. The soldiers had "dug" in, but there was almost no combat activity. They were encircled, but both sides did nothing. To keep the German soldiers busy, their officers loaned them to the SS, who were combing the nearby forest for Latvian and German deserters, as well as for escaped Jews.

Through Anton we found out that all the Dundaga camps and also the Poperwalen camp had been marched to Libau, a distance of about 140 kilometers. During that march, consisting of over five thousand Jews, of whom two-thirds were Hungarian and the rest the "old timers" from the ghetto, both Latvian and German, about one hundred of the Latvian Jews had escaped. Most of them were caught quickly, brought to Talsi, and shot there. Others held out for quite a while until they, too, were discovered. Only a handful were lucky enough to see freedom.

The winter months presented a new problem for us: The attic became bitter cold. As the supply of hay for the animals started to dwindle, we had to use some burlap bags that Anton brought. Matis and I talked a lot in order to forget the cold and the danger of being discovered. Klara told us one day that the German soldiers had discovered two Jews in the dairy plant not far away. They handed them over the to the Latvians and their fate was sealed in Talsi.

By April the situation started to change in a subtle way. We heard the soldiers discussing the certainty of being taken prisoners by the Russians, and we heard from Klara that many little boats were leaving the harbor, carrying Latvians to Sweden. Most of them had been on very friendly terms with the Germans and had much to fear from the Soviets.

Then, on May 8, at noon, when the sun was at its highest point, Anton and Klara came into the barn and did not even bother to close the door behind them. Anton told us solemnly that he had just listened to the radio and heard that the Germans had signed the papers of capitulation! Hitler was dead! All of Germany was occupied by the Allies! We embraced each other and thanked God for permitting us to live. Then, the next day, May 9, we listened as Marshall Stalin told the Russian people that they had won and that the war was over!

It had taken us many years and much suffering, and now these last three hundred days were over too, thanks to such good people as Anton, Klara, and Skaidrite Vanags!

EDITOR'S NOTE

Abraham or Abrasha Shpungin has lived in Israel since 1971. He is currently working on his memoirs, entitled *"Dos is doch geven asoi"* from which these vignettes are culled. He is also active in the Association of Jews from Latvia and Estonia.

After his liberation in 1945, he went back to his native Jēkabpils and found out that his parents and brothers had been murdered by the Arajs *Kommando* at the swamps of Kukas. Among the murderers were erstwhile neighbors.

Mr. Shpungin finished university training with a degree in chemistry. He married Shelly Bers and they have two sons, Alexander and Reuven. When the Shpungins applied for a visa to Israel, in 1968, both of them lost their jobs and encountered many difficulties before being permitted to leave in 1971. In Israel, Abraham worked at the Weizmann Institute until his retirement in 1987, and Shelly worked at a laboratory connected with a hospital. Their sons are well established and they have four grandchildren.

Abraham Shpungin has remained in touch with the Vanags family ever since his liberation. He is also in touch with Matis Frost, who lives in Rishon LeZion, Israel. Both men testified when Gustav Sorge was indicted, but they were not permitted to leave Latvia to give their testimony in person.

Despite his harrowing experiences and the death of his loved ones, Abrasha Shpungin is not bitter. He feels, however, that none of these tales should be lost so that the world will remember what was done to innocent people for no other reason than the fact that they were Jewish.

13

And I Almost Did Not Make It

Rita Wassermann

March 9, 1945. We were told to line up, take whatever we "owned"—obviously an attempt at humor—and get ready to leave. We had very little strength left and we did not know what awaited us. But there was nothing to do but follow orders and so we left the camp in Gotentov (Godętowo) at 6:00 in the evening and went on a march that was to last the whole night and half a day.

March 10, 1945. We reached Chinov (Chynowie). According to rumors, we were supposed to go to the coast where a boat was waiting. The barn in Chinov, into which we were ordered to go, was a place to rest for a while. It was filled with Jews, alive and dead, and in addition to them, there were also live and dead horses; people soon started to cut up the latter. Hunger hurts.

My sister had been ill for the last few days and especially so during the long night. She was burning up with fever and my mother and I literally pulled her along, holding her from both sides, since anyone who fell was killed instantly. We were cold, hungry, wet and tired and worst of all, without hope.

Not too long after our arrival at the barn, my mother, standing at the big gate, began yelling, "Children, the Russians . . . the Russians are here . . . we are going to be free!" I thought my mother had gone crazy and I asked God, "What do I do now? My sister is ill and my mother is crazy!"

But the Russians were really in Chinov and mother started crying. She ran out of the barn and grabbed the first Russian soldier she saw. She hugged him and kept repeating, "You saved my children, you saved my children, thank you, thank you."

Suddenly, my sister walked out of the barn and went over to a parked German truck that was loaded with sugar. Burning up with fever, she took control of it and would let no one near it. Finally my mother convinced her that she could not keep the truck and that she had better come down. Before abandoning the truck, my sister took off her little green, wet, dirty cap and filled it with sugar. She was keeping it no matter what, and she held onto it and would not let go of it as if her life depended on it. But then she and I and mother, as well as many others, stood and watched the roundup of the SS men and their immediate execution. Among them was our commandant.

To us, however, the Russians were rather nice. They permitted a few of us to go into the spacious house on the hill behind the barn and gave us food. Unfortunately, many people who ate too much or too fast died because they were not used to eating. What a night! The beds were soft and there were clean sheets and blankets, but I could not fall asleep. After much tossing and turning, I finally took a thin, dirty blanket and fell asleep on the cold stone floor within two minutes. Others seemed to have the same trouble. How sad! We were not used to soft beds, clean sheets, and other normal comforts of life.

The next day it was time to move on again because we were too near the front lines. As usual, my mother took charge. First she got some clothes for us since ours were dirty, wet, and infested with lice. She also got some shoes for us, and best of all, she managed to get two horses and a wagon. We were free—really free—and we were on our way. My mother deserves all the credit. My sister and I and several others as well would not have survived the camps and the first couple of months of freedom without my mother's ingenuity and resourcefulness.

There were twelve of us on the wagon. As we traveled through the woods, some former partisans stopped us and took one of our precious horses. For a while everyone walked; only two women who were terribly sick were allowed to ride. My sister was driving the horses. She knew very little about it, but somehow she managed. Eventually, we found another horse and then all of us could ride on the wagon. Every day we traveled for a few hours and then we stopped for the night in a barn. We were very weak and some of us were ill, myself included. I got dysentery so badly that it was often too late before I could get to a proper place. God, what a time! We traveled from village to village, at first west, and then south.

Along the way, we encountered many people who did not want to help us. Germans, Poles, and the *Volksdeutsche* of Pomerania evidently still hated the Jews. In some cases they did not allow us to spend the night in their barns and did so only when they were forced to by the Russians. Yet, there were some people who did try to help. They felt sorry for us. We all looked awful, just walking skin and bones.

At one point, we just could not go any further. We had reached a formerly magnificent estate. In one part of the large manor, the Russians had set up some sort of headquarters. They permitted us to stay in what had been a large dining room, provided those of us who could worked on the neglected farm. My mother became the cook for the officers and for a while I was well enough to take care of the cows together with two of the other girls. I did such a good job that the Russian officer in charge said they would take me back to Russia once they left. We were terribly agitated.

As it turned out however, we need not have worried, for I got violently ill—I had evidently caught the typhoid fever from which my sister was just recuperating. The Russian officer was furious and made all of us leave in order to avoid infecting his men. One of them helped my sister to put the horses in harness and we were on our way again.

April 12, 1945. We had to leave four of the women in a hospital, since it was clear that they were too ill to travel. A car pulled up next to our wagon and a political officer with a red star on his cap told us that in far away America "good President Roosevelt" had died. My mother told him a little bit about us and it turned out that he was Jewish. He brought a doctor to look at me and gave me some medicine. Although the doctor felt I would be better off in a hospital, we did not want to be separated and so he let us go. The medicine helped to bring down the fever and I soon felt better.

April 20, 1945. As we were driving on a nice quiet road, we were stopped by a Russian officer, who told us that if we kept on traveling this very road, we would soon be able to say "Happy Birthday" to Hitler. My sister convinced the horses to turn around quickly and took another road, one that brought us to Konitz (Chojnice). We found out that the trains were running, but before we boarded one, my clever mother sold the horses and the wagon to a Polish farmer!

Our train ride was complicated. First stop Bromberg (Bydgoszcz), then Thorn (Toruń), and then, since there was yet no way to go south in a straight line, we went southeast. We passed through the rubble that was once Warsaw, then to Lublin, to Chelm, and ended up in Lemberg (Lvov). We were now a transport, consisting of some Russians, a few Poles, Hungarians, Jews, and gypsies. Two young gypsy brothers, Franz and Rudi, were originally from Austria. They were very scared of the Russians and kept close to my mother. Actually, we were like gypsies too, but it did not matter; all we wanted was to go back to Vienna any way we could. (We had made plans with my father, Pinkas Hirschhorn, to meet him there.)

After Lvov we went south again. In the town of Stryj we found some kind Jews and they let us take a bath in a real tub—the first such luxury since our deportation from Vienna in February 1942! My skin was blotched and ugly and I thought I would be scarred for life. The nice lady who had taken us in spent hours dressing my skin with a medicated salve and thanks to her, my skin eventually became white and flawless.

After two days of bliss we boarded yet another train. We passed through Munkács (Mukačevo) and Uzgorod.

May 9, 1945. The train stopped in the little town of Čop. Suddenly, the Russians yelled, "Everybody out, everybody out! The war is over! The war is over!"

It is hard to describe what followed. The train station became the most perfect place for a wonderful party. We celebrated, and there was singing, dancing, laughter, and then the gypsies started playing. To this day I don't know where they got their violins from and how there were so many of them. As they played, the tears came, but even so, it was the most unforgettable party of my life!

We passed through Kaschau (Košice), where some of the Hungarians who had been with us in Riga left us, and then, finally, we arrived in Budapest. Although there was much evidence of fighting, it was a totally different world.

They still had a Jewish Community Center, and we were made welcome. We were among the first to return from the East, and they tried very hard to make up for our suffering, even though they knew that material things would not do it. But it felt good to be coddled, at least for a while. We stayed in Budapest for two weeks. My sister celebrated her seventeenth birthday on May 27 and full of hope and cheer we left for Vienna.

June 1, 1945. After a two-day journey, passing through well-remembered vacation spots of long ago such as Stein-am-Anger (Szombathely) and Ödenburg (Sopron), we arrived in Vienna. We said good-bye to

Rudi and Franz at the Süd-Ost Bahnhof (southeast station) and went directly to the Jewish *Kultusgemeinde* now at 25 Schottenring, hoping to find my father or news about him. No such luck. Here, too, we were among the first to come back from the East, but Vienna's Jews had almost all been sent away, and so they were not as well equipped to take care of returnees as the Jews from Budapest had been. They put us for a few nights in what had been a former Jewish school next to the ruins of a temple, and again my mother got busy. Since our pre-Hitler apartment was in the suburbs and presently occupied, she demanded and got the apartment of my father's aunt whose maid had denounced her but had fled when the Russians arrived. Since it stood empty, was easily accessible, and we were the only surviving family, we stayed there until the day when we left the city for good.

A few days after we moved in, we had a big surprise: About twenty or so gypsies came to our apartment, laden with food and flowers; it was the family of Rudi and Franz and they wanted to thank my mother for bringing the boys home safely. We had a great party!

Several weeks went by and we sadly realized that nothing had changed in Vienna. They still did not like the Jews, but now they would not admit it. On the contrary, everybody had had a Jewish relative or a Jewish friend who "went away." No one had any idea what had happened to the Jews or what Hitler had done to them; silently they all felt that whatever had been done had been necessary.

We tried to resume a normal lifestyle, but it was very difficult. My mother saw to it that we had food and my sister started taking all kinds of courses, but I was at odds with myself. I was depressed and as I walked around Vienna, the city of my birth, my so-called home, I looked into faces and wondered, "Were you and you and you one of those who tortured, maimed, and ultimately killed us?" I was then very young, not yet fifteen, but I had seen too much and had suffered too much. I no longer knew how to trust. I was free, but I was not happy.

One day I awoke and was not feeling well. I had no idea what was wrong, but I did not feel up to par. After a while my back exploded with a fierce pain and I passed out. A doctor came and said that I had gravel in the kidney; I passed the gravel and felt fine.

July 18, 1945. My father's forty-seventh birthday. It was two weeks after I had passed out and now, suddenly, I had a very high temperature. My mother called the same doctor and at first he thought it was related to the earlier kidney problem. Although I was delirious, I was also very scared, since illness to me meant not only doctor and hospital, but death. In the camps when someone was ill, he or she was soon killed. The doctor insisted that I had to go to the hospital for tests and I was taken to the Jewish hospital only a few blocks from where we lived. This time I had another strain of typhoid fever and it was life threatening. I was put in isolation, and it soon became clear that there were horrendous complications, such as a mild form of polio.

Different forms of treatment were tried, but nothing seemed to work. Americans who had come to Vienna on June 19—up to then there had only been the Russians who had taken the city—tried to help me by offering the new wonder drug penicillin. As it turned out, I was allergic to it.

Most of the time I did not know what was going on; only sometimes I thought I saw my mother sitting next to my bed. Evidently, despite the isolation, they could not keep her away from me. She constantly put compresses on my feverish head and massaged my legs.

August 30, 1945. It was my fifteenth birthday and I didn't even know it.

After that I got better, but I could not walk at all and I was very weak. At least they moved me to a room with other people, and I was allowed to have visitors.

In the meantime, we were still hoping for my father to come back. Everyday people came back from Buchenwald. It was hard to cross into Lower Austria, since it was the Russian Zone; yet they came. One day, my good friend Leo Granierer came back; he had met someone at the station who told him where I was. He knew nothing about my father, or so he said, but I knew well where his mother was . . . she had visited me just a day earlier and was supposed to come again.

I told him he would soon see her, but I did not want to shock her. So he went for a short walk and when she came in, together with my mother and sister, I asked her what she would do if Leo would walk in right now. She started to cry and said that it would be the best day of her life, but that so far she did not know whether he had survived those last, terrible months. All of us tried to calm her down.

Then she said to me, "Rita, you are so peculiar today . . . are you running a fever again? You must concentrate on getting better!"

Just then, Leo walked in. It is impossible to describe the reunion of mother and son, finding each other alive. A true miracle in these bad times. We needed miracles.

That evening, the fever soared again. At first the doctor thought it was the excitement, but then he found out that the lady in the bed next to me had given me some fresh tomatoes from her garden, brought in by her husband. They pumped out my stomach, but it was too late. I had a relapse and was moved into isolation once again.

Professor Donat, my physician, told my mother that there was little hope and that he was not at all sure of my surviving this third bout of typhoid fever. He said, "I know you brought her out of hell . . . I have tried everything I know . . . but I fear the worst."

My indomitable mother, however, did not give up. She went to speak to an officer at the Russian headquarters in Vienna's second district, gave him two watches for a bottle of vodka, and then, with Professor Donat's permission, proceeded to sponge my body with a mixture of vodka and lukewarm water. From time to time, she dribbled some of the mixture into my mouth and made me swallow it. She did this for a whole night, and in the morning the fever was down and I was on the way to recovery.

It was a long road. Fall and winter passed. I got therapy, and very slowly my legs started to come back to life, and I relearned how to walk. I always had visitors, but the one person for whom I waited never came. I hoped and prayed for my father's return, but it was all in vain. He had been killed on the very day that Buchenwald was liberated.

June 4, 1946. I was allowed to go home. We celebrated with a small party. A few of our friends were there, among them Mrs. Leah Granierer and her son Leo. She was one happy lady, holding onto his hand. She is gone now, as is my beloved mother. I will always miss Mama, but I guess when I compare myself to those who lost everyone, I am rather lucky, for I came out of the camps not only with my mother, but with my sister as well.

Only half a year after I came home from the hospital, the three of us left for the United States. It took some time to get used to a new country, to a new homeland, but Vienna could never be home again because my father did not come back.

It took me twenty-five years before I got up the courage to return to Vienna for a visit, mainly to see the Granierers. The city was as beautiful as ever, but when I walked the streets, memories—not very beautiful, to be sure—walked with me. People say that it is time to forgive and forget. I can't.

EDITOR'S NOTE

According to official records, five thousand Viennese Jews were sent to Riga. The first transport was shunted to Kovno, where all one thousand were murdered on November 29, 1941. Of the four thousand who subsequently went to Riga, fifty-nine came back, among them my mother, my sister, and I. Rita is the youngest to survive . . . she was eleven when we reached the ghetto. As she points out in her story, she celebrated her fifteenth birthday in Vienna, free at last, "and did not even know it." I remember her lying in the hospital bed, shrunken and pale, and always asking, "Did you hear anything about Papa?"

Her bouts with typhus and polio cast a pall over our relief at having been liberated. After her health returned and we left for the United States, Rita refused for many years to talk about what she had suffered, both psychologically in regard to my father's death, as well as physically. It is only now that she permits others a glimpse of her pain.

She and her husband live in the New York area; she has a son and a daughter as well as two granddaughters. Rita works for the Professional Staff Congress of the City University of New York and is truly liked by whoever comes in contact with her.

Recently the Austrian government advertised that we, the survivors, would finally be eligible to receive a pension. Up to now, Austrian Jews, in contrast to German Jews, did not receive restitution. However, the law indicated that one had to be fifteen years by May 9, 1945, in order to qualify. My sister's case was therefore rejected, since she had her fifteenth birthday three months later. As she writes: "Nothing had changed in Vienna . . ." and I can only add: "Nothing ever will!"

14

A Daughter Remembers

Eleonora Storch Schwab

In 1952, my father, Hilel Storch, was awarded the Order of Vasa (First Class) by the King of Sweden, Gustav V. Although the certificate gives no reason for this honor, I assume that he received the medal for his humanitarian efforts during World War II.

My first recollections of father's activities go back to the bleak years of 1944 and 1945. At the time we lived in Stockholm at Furusundsgatan 10, and I remember the sound of phones ringing late at night and long conversations in Swedish, Russian, Yiddish, and German. I also remember my mother staying up until the wee hours of the morning, waiting for father to return from meetings. Names I became familiar with included Nazi leaders such as Adolf Hitler, Heinrich Himmler, Ernst Kaltenbrunner, and Peter Kleist, father's friend Mr. Klaus, Himmler's Masseur Felix Kersten, and Swedish personalities such as Tage Erlander, Count Folke Bernadotte, and Raoul Wallenberg.

Born in 1902 in Dvinsk (Daugavpils), Latvia, father became involved in Zionist activities at an early age. At the age of eighteen he represented the Jewish Agency, which, prior to the creation of the State of Israel, was considered to be the "Jewish government" of Palestine. In Dvinsk and later in Riga, to which he moved for business reasons in the 1920s, he helped promote the emigration of some three thousand Jews from Latvia to Palestine.

As a businessman he established excellent connections in Sweden. He left Riga for Stockholm in 1940, leaving my mother Anna and me behind. Hardly had he touched Swedish soil, when he was arrested. A foreigner with an obsessive style, he did not fit the relaxed Swedish mold or stereotype and was suspected of engaging in activities not in the interest of Sweden. He was kept in custody for four days. It was in this context that he met the future prime minister of the country, Tage Erlander, who, at the time of father's incarceration, was in charge of the police and who later became a close friend of the family.

His status as a foreigner with a police record notwithstanding, he left no stone unturned to get mother and me out of Riga. As I understand it, there was talk between Stockholm and Moscow regarding the exchange of a spy; mother and I were made part of a package deal and we reached Stockholm by plane in May 1941, shortly before the Nazi invasion of the Soviet Union.

Following the invasion, father, as the political representative of the Jewish Agency in Sweden (until Israel opened its embassy in Stockholm in the early 1950s) and as the representative of the World Jewish Congress, sprang into action. But this was not very easy. Jews in general were not that popular, and the Swedish Jews themselves were not very well disposed toward father. Disbelieving the magnitude of the German crimes and fearful that a mass influx of Jews to Sweden would engender anti-Semitism, much of the Jewish community in Sweden viewed father not only with great suspicion, but also with alarm. An incident often told at home bears mentioning and illustrates the point; pregnant with my brother Marcus, mother, accompanied by father, went to the synagogue on Wahrendorfsgatan. Father asked that a seat be vacated for his pregnant wife and was told "Storch's wife can stand."

Many years later, I read in the extensive literature about father's belief in 1942 and 1943 that the Germans had resorted to the mass murder of Jews. At the time, however, being only four years old, I do not remember anything unusual happening at home. It was not until the summer of 1944 in Falsterbo, a resort town in the south of Sweden, that I recollect mother crying all the time. By that time my brother Marcus was two years old, my new sister Ruth was not yet one, and very often the three of us were whisked our of our rented summer home, apparently in order not to see mother in that state of despair. Our Swedish governess Vera Olsson, an amateur violinist, took us for what I considered never-ending walks. Much later I found out the reason for mother's behavior. She had learned that the members of her family who had remained in Latvia had been brutally murdered by the Nazis and their

Latvian collaborators. Members of my father's family too had been butchered by then.

Back in Stockholm from a lovely summer at the shores of the Strait of Kattegat, I was soon struck by father's frequent absences and the little time he spent with his children. I often heard mother exclaiming that last night father returned at two, at three, or even at four. Among the earliest visitors to our apartment, I remember Akim Spivak, Leon Lapidus, and chief rabbi of Sweden, Marcus Ehrenpreis. All were prominent members of the Swedish Jewish community and curious about what was transpiring, I often slipped out of my room to look and listen.

As far as I was concerned, the most interesting visitor was our handsome neighbor, Mr. Edgar Klaus. Apparently originally from Riga, much mystery surrounded him. Although he was Jewish, at one point he was suspected of being a double agent, working for Nazi Germany as well as for the Soviet Union. Actually, he was negotiating with the Nazis on behalf of the Soviets. He even traveled to Germany. I eventually found out that the substance of his negotiations concerned a separate peace between the two arch foes. It was this Mr. Klaus who on one occasion returned from Germany with a banana for the Storch children. It was divided into three parts and I remember that I did not like it much. The exotic fruit had turned mushy. At the time, bananas were not available in Sweden and my parents appreciated the gesture more than we did.

Mr. Klaus's visits were usually lengthy ones. He talked to father about matters he had learned in Germany, and I remember several times when father got very excited about important information. The end of Mr. Klaus was a sad one. If memory serves me right, I believe that he took his own life. I remember my father returning from Klaus's apartment and saying, "My God, my God . . ."

Early in 1945, I became aware of all the activities' gathering momentum. There were many late night calls to and from Germany. Father, the activist, emerged as the most prominent Jew in neutral Sweden, with easy access to the king, prime minister, and leading politicians. He received a very important letter from Count Folke Bernadotte, the nephew of Sweden's king and, in his own right, the vice-president of the Swedish Red Cross. The letter is dated February 26, 1945 and states:

Because of Swiss intervention, a few thousand Jews have been permitted to leave for Switzerland. According to authorities in Berlin, this undertaking is continuing and additional Jews could, conceivably, leave Germany by way of Switzerland. As you know, serious attempts have been made by Swedish authorities to obtain permission for some Jews to leave for Sweden as well. On my last visit to Berlin a few days ago, I was able to verify that this question is viewed favorably, even if no definite answer could yet be elicited.

True to his style, father was anxious to exploit this opening. But why father? That Count Bernadotte should have written to him was not surprising. Both had been working toward the same goal . . . to save lives. With the war rapidly drawing to an end, there were Nazis in high places who were eager to terminate it in such a way that they would emerge unscathed. One plan entailed ending the war in the West while keeping it going in the East. Since father's connections reached all the way up to the White House by way of the founder and president of the World Jewish Congress, Rabbi Steven Wise, it was perhaps natural for some of the well-informed Nazis to think that by turning to him they could obtain their goal and simultaneously save their skin.

Shortly before receiving the communication from the count, father was made aware that he might be invited to visit Berlin—secretely, of course. But who among the Nazi leaders would or could enter into substantive negotiations with a Jew about saving Jewish lives? It turned out that it was no less a figure than the dreaded *Reichsfuehrer SS*, Heinrich Himmler, perhaps the most vicious member of Hitler's trusted entourage, who invited father! The invitation was transmitted to father in the form of a letter written by Felix Kersten, Himmler's masseur, on April 4, 1945: "Dear Mr. Storch, Attempted to reach you by phone, but to no avail. I am therefore writing these lines in haste. . . . Himmler will only be available on Saturday. We must therefore fly on Saturday morning, at the very latest."

In close touch with Kersten, without whose medical ministrations Himmler was often unable to function, father had ascertained that Himmler, without Hitler's knowledge, was prepared to release Jews in return for the Allies' ceasing to bomb Germany, at least temporarily. He was even prepared to establish contact with the Western Allies in order to capitulate to them. Father, of course, was in no position to make any commitments. But at least there was an opening to deal with this demon.

But father, a Jew, in Hitler's Germany, in the company of Himmler? Furthermore, father, not being a citizen of Sweden, could not even legally claim Swedish protection on Nazi soil. Yet, determined and stubborn as usual, he was ready to go.

Himmler's assurance of father's safety notwithstanding, mother finally put her foot down. She objected to being left alone with three small children and, as I have been told over and over again, hid his identification papers. Unable to sway her, and also doubtful of being able to accomplish any more than had already been done, father sent Norbert Masur, a prominent member of the Swedish Jewish community, in his stead.

But why Masur and not Fritz Hollander, another prominent member of Sweden's Jewish community? After all, Masur had little knowledge of the intricate negotiations that had been going on for some time, whereas Hollander was somewhat better informed. What struck me as a nearly seven-year-old child sounds funny today but made a big impression on me at the time. Father's choice of Masur was based on the latter's bearing. Between the two, father felt that Masur looked more mature. Not as good looking as Hollander and appearing older than his age because, and this was critical to me, of his moustache, father thought that Himmler would take him more seriously.

In view of the far-reaching accord that had already been worked out in March 1945, Masur's very dangerous visit was, as father had anticipated correctly, anticlimactic.

According to a carefully orchestrated plan by Father, Himmler and Kersten both signed an agreement in Germany on March 12. Point one stated "That I (Himmler) will not convey the Fuehrer's orders to blow up concentration camps with all the inmates in the face of the approaching Allies. I forbid any kind of destruction, including the killing of prisoners." Point two provided "That in the face of the approaching Allies, concentration camps are to be turned over in an orderly fashion with white flags." Point three stated "That any further killing of Jews must cease and be forbidden, and that Jews must be put on an equal footing with other concentration camp inmates." The fourth and last point stated "That concentration camps must not be evacuated and that inmates be kept in place, and that all prisoners are to be permitted to receive food parcels from Sweden."

Despite this agreement, a major tragedy was about to occur. Peter Kleist, an aide to Nazi Foreign Minister von Ribbentrop, informed Father on April 7, 1945, that Kaltenbrunner, a rival of Himmler in the bizarre politics among Hitler's cohorts, had issued an order to Eichmann to have Bergen Belsen blown up at 6:00 A.M. on the following day. In Father's presence, Kersten telephoned Himmler. He spoke to the latter's adjutant Rudolf Brandt about the need to stop Kaltenbrunner, if the agreement that he and Himmler had signed on March 12 was to have any meaning. Father meanwhile phoned Count Bernadotte, who was then in Germany. Bernadotte immediately contacted Brandt and other leading Nazis in an effort to stop this crime.

The tragedy was averted at the very last moment. To check the intrigues of Kaltenbrunner, who was endeavoring to undermine Himmler's standing with Hitler, Himmler appointed several Nazis who were loyal to him, and they made sure that no one was either evacuated or killed in Bergen Belsen. Although Himmler had agreed to let the prisoners receive food parcels, they were not given any, and they starved to death. On the other hand, there is no doubt that many survived who would otherwise have been killed.

On Count Bernadotte's return to Sweden, he wrote to Father on April 17, 1945, about Himmler's repeated reassurance that no camp would be blown up. He especially mentioned Theresienstadt, Bergen Belsen, and Buchenwald. (Although Bergen Belsen had indeed been handed over intact on April 14, the Buchenwald authorities, on April 8, had evacuated nearly thirty thousand Jews, of whom twenty-six thousand died within the next two weeks. Buchenwald was liberated on April 11, one week *before* Bernadotte wrote his letter to Hilel Storch. *The Editor.*)

The Talmud states that when a person saves another person's life, it is like saving the world. Though much remains to be said of Father's activities during and after the cessation of hostilities—including the seventy thousand or so food parcels that he secured and sent to concentration camp inmates, his endeavors to reunite families who had survived the Holocaust, and his later activities on behalf of Jews in Palestine (in order to ensure the viability of Israel, he was involved in smuggling arms and ammunition to the new State)—here I would merely like to conclude my remarks by briefly summarizing what had been accomplished as far as saving lives was concerned, Father's primary objective during those frightful years.

Because of his efforts, even before the war ended, the records show that almost eight thousand Jews were brought to Sweden, and immediately after the armistice, an additional eight thousand arrived, close to death. In fact, over one thousand died despite all efforts and were buried in different parts of the country.

In addition, as a result of Father's agreements with Himmler and the latter's promise not to blow up the concentration camps or kill their inhabitants, untold Jewish lives were saved. If Himmler's orders had not been sabotaged by local SS, or countermanded by Kaltenbrunner, many more could have survived. Father tried everything in his power and he succeeded; many of the survivors who lived to see freedom and rejoiced in their ''good luck'' had no idea that a man named Storch was the cause of their happiness.

Although not of the same scope as his rescue activities, but certainly in the spirit of the Talmud, I remember Father telling me on numerous occasions that with the help of a permit elicited by him from the Swedish government, 350 "Turks" were allowed to land in Göteborg in 1944. In reality, these Turks were Polish Jews whom the Jewish Agency had managed to save. After only a two-day stay in Sweden, they left for Palestine. I believe it was also in that same year that father was involved in bringing fifty-five Norwegian Jews of mixed marriages to Sweden.

Another recollection deals with the Jews in Finland. Both Hitler and Himmler demanded that Field Marshal Mannerheim turn over all foreign Jews to Germany. Mannerheim refused. However, due to this precarious situation both for Finnish as well as for foreign jews, a delegation of Finnish Jews arrived from Helsinki and visited father. Deeply concerned by what he was told, father immediately contacted Tage Erlander, who was then minister of state. Father received the promise that if the situation were to warrant it, Erlander would bring the Jews of Finland to Sweden. This never came to pass, as Mannerheim successfully resisted the Nazis' demand.

On Father's seventieth birthday in June 1972, the prime minister of Sweden wrote him the following letter:

Brother:

We met a long time ago, when I was still a student and you had recently come to our country. Already then I felt the meaningful contributions you were making to save Jewish lives from the Nazi atrocities. It was a significant contribution to humanity. Since then I have had the pleasure of often discussing with you a variety of world political questions.

On your seventieth birthday I would like to congratulate you and express my appreciation for your contributions as well as convey my best wishes for your continuing intensive activities.

With kindest regards, I remain your devoted

Olaf Palme

Eleven years later, when father died in 1983, Prime Minister Palme wrote the following obituary in the *Stockholm Tidningen:*

Hilel Storch In Memoriam

My friendship with Hilel Storch had an unusual origin. An uncle of mine had a serious hip complaint. He came to Sweden from Riga, and was treated for his hip by a masseur by the name of Felix Kersten, who was attributed almost miraculous qualities. Among his patients were the Queen Dowager

Wilhelmina of Holland and the Chief of the Gestapo, Heinrich Himmler. Whilst in Riga, my uncle had made the acquaintance of a Jewish businessman called Hilel Storch who later fled to Sweden from Nazism and Communism. It was here that they renewed their friendship.

Towards the end of the war I was invited to tea at my uncle's house. Among the other guests were Felix Kersten and Hilel Storch. Kersten was enormously fat, and I remember how greedily he ate orange marmalade direct from the bowl. Storch was a little, quiet man. The conversation revolved around how one could save Jews from concentration camps and if Kersten could influence Himmler in this direction. Himmler was considered to be greatly dependent upon Kersten. I don't intend to go any deeper into the respective roles played by Folke Bernadotte, and Kersten and Storch. That is something for historians. However, it is a well-known fact that many Jews were saved from the concentration camps at the last minute, and that Storch played an important role in that respect.

Later, he became the representative in Sweden of the World Jewish Congress, and a close friend of Nahum Goldmann. I had conversations with him when he used to visit Prime Minister Tage Erlander and he visited me regularly during my period as prime minister and party leader. He had a broad outlook concerning the status of Jews in the world, and a deep insight amongst other things through his friendship with Goldmann. Later on, when he became ill but felt he still had many things to accomplish, he used to contact me almost every week.

Now he is no more. I felt great affection for him. He has left behind him a memory of a friendly, vital person with a burning desire to safeguard the interests of the Jews. But also with strong ties to Sweden where he once found a place of refuge. Therefore I think it is important to pay tribute to him.

The German philosopher Hegel is reputed to have said that sometimes it is difficult to distinguish where tragedy ends and comedy begins. To celebrate his victory, Hitler was going to build a monument of huge granite blocks that he had ordered from Sweden. When father learned after the war that they were stored in Bohuslän, Sweden, he purchased the granite stones, using funds raised in South Africa, in Argentina, and his own money as well. Then, with the financial help of the Polish government, the blocks were transported to Warsaw and there Hegel's words about the tragicomedy came true: Storch, the Jew, turned the dream of a victory monument by history's most evil man into a memorial for Hitler's Jewish victims as well as into a symbol of Jewish heroism in the face of annihilation. Located on the blood-soaked grounds of the Warsaw ghetto, it had a plaque that stated that the monument was donated by the Swedish section of the World Jewish Congress. (The Poles eventually removed the plaque!)

It is perhaps no accident that in addition to Yom Kippur, the day that meant most to Father as I remember, was the commemoration of the Warsaw ghetto uprising. Just two weeks before his death, with his last strength, Father went to the Warsaw ghetto memorial that was held at the synagogue in Stockholm. Ill and frail, he fell several times and had to be picked up from the floor. Stubborn as always, he refused to give in and leave. With black and blue marks all over his body, he was finally taken home and to the hospital, where he died on April 25, 1983. Shortly before his death, he was anxious for Prime Minister Palme to visit him in the hospital, so that he could explain why the prime minister should under no circumstances receive Yasir Arafat. But death interrupted father's last wish.

EDITOR'S NOTE

When I asked Eleonora Schwab to write a vignette about her late father, Hilel Storch, she replied, "So many books and articles about my father have already been written. . . . why would you want another one?" I said, "Not one of the authors knew him the way you did!" After thinking about it for a while, Eleonora agreed to write down what she remembered about those desperate days. It was not easy for her; she is a very private person. She realized, however, that her father was so unique among men, such a driven personality when it came to saving his people, that a daughter's loving memories were sorely needed to flesh out the events of that time.

The bibliography of this volume contains the books that have been written about Hilel Storch. I remember meeting him at the Bar Mitzvah of the Schwab triplets. The place was the beautiful Lincoln Center Synagogue and there stood the proud grandfather, joining in the ancient prayers, a Jew among Jews, and a prince among men!

His grandsons have grown up, he has passed away, Eleonora and her husband, Professor George Schwab, are active in various fields, among them the Jewish Survivors of Latvia, but those of us who survived the Holocaust will never cease to be grateful to Hilel Storch, whose endeavors saved so many of his people.

15

Epilogue

Gertrude Schneider

It is done. I have kept my promise. The tragedy that befell the Jews of
Latvia and those many foreign Jews brought to that country has been
recorded in three volumes, of which *The Unfinished Road* is the last.

Even my clever father, Pinkas Hirschhorn, could not have imagined
that my childish diary would eventually become the seed for such a
trilogy. When he asked me to keep a proper record and write down
important events, he set in motion a process that has led to my resolve
of becoming the chronicler of two very different Jewish groups that
were destined to share a common fate.

I started on this labor of love and duty shortly after the end of the
war, as soon as I arrived back in my native Vienna. In early 1946, my
description of our deportation to Riga entitled *Fahrt ins Grauen* was
published, and it led to my being called as a witness against the man in
charge of the Jewish deportation process in Austria. His name was Anton Brunner.

At his trial I also mentioned Alois Brunner (no relation), one of Anton's associates. Alois Brunner had been our transport commander on
the way to Riga. I had no idea at the time that our reception at the
freight terminal in Skirotava was staged by the local *Sicherheitsdienst*
to give him a glimpse of how to deal with deportees, since he was being
groomed to become the official in charge of Jewish deportation in sev-

eral European countries. The Dortmund transport, which had arrived in Riga on February 1, 1942, was supposed to have been the last one. Yet, about three hundred of us were permitted to walk into the ghetto. The other seven hundred were urged to take the buses "since the walk was far and they could, in that way, prepare a place for those who did the walking." The buses brought them to the Bikernieku Forest, where graves, measuring eight meters by eight meters and four meters deep, had already been prepared.

At any rate, while Anton Brunner was sentenced to death for crimes against humanity, and was duly hanged in May of 1946, Alois Brunner managed to flee to Syria where he still resides, basking in the glory of bygone days.

I came to the United States in 1947 and immediately began a new life by going to school. I had already lost too many years. At that time I gave little thought to increasing the world's knowledge of the Holocaust in Latvia, especially since I was familiar with the two volumes written about it. One was *Die Vernichtung der Juden Lettlands* by Max Kaufmann, solely from the perspective of Latvian Jews, and the other one, *Sadismus oder Wahnsinn* by Jeanette Wolff, from the perspective of German Jews. While some of what they had written made me feel uncomfortable and although certain facts did not agree with what I had written in my own diary on the days when the actual events occurred, I was more or less content to leave everything to them.

While still in the ghetto of Riga, both of them were already middle-aged and saw some of the events in a different light. I did feel, while reading their books, that each of them could have said more about the other group with whom they had shared that inhospitable place.

Kaufmann had lost his wife Franka in the December 8, 1941 massacre and his son Arthur at the peat bogs of Sloka on May 20, 1943. His extraordinary opus reflected his pain. The book contained a myriad of details, which he had collected on little slips of paper immediately after the war and which he then recorded faithfully, adding names wherever possible. Seldom, however, did he mention any of the deportees by name. In fact, whenever he did mention German Jews, one could sense criticism and a lingering distrust.

In later years, after I had done my own research, I spoke to him about it. Although I could never change his mind, he respected me as a scholar, so much so that he asked me to include the story of his son's murder in *Muted Voices,* the second volume of the trilogy.

Jeanette Wolff lost her husband and her youngest daughter in Riga. Her oldest daughter was killed in the concentration camp Ravensbrück.

Only her daughter Edith, who was together with her, survived the war and, like her mother, remained in Germany.

In her book, Jeanette Wolff mentions the Latvian Jews and their martyrdom several times, but very briefly. The German Jews and their suffering were her main concern. There are many important details contained in her opus, but she was not too concerned with exact dates and numbers. When I visited her in Berlin in 1971, I told her that while I appreciated what she had written, I wished that she had given the proper dates and also the numbers of people being sent to various places. She did not think it was all that important and felt content that I would set the record straight. She was very supportive of my efforts to learn more and her connections in Germany, as a former member of the *Bundestag,* opened many doors for me, giving me access to records that I might otherwise not have seen.

Pursuing a doctorate in history at the Graduate School of the City University of New York, I majored in modern European history, with a minor in medieval history. During my second term, I wrote a paper on the German ghetto in Riga. My professor, an Irishman by the name of William O. Shanahan, was astonished. He knew much about the Jewish destruction in Europe, but he had never realized the perfection with which it was accomplished. He was very touched and advised me to make the subject my eventual dissertation.

My lecture after that class was in medieval history. I was early, but the professor was there already. He asked me the reason for my obvious excitement and I told him what his colleague had said to me. The rest, to use a pun, is history: That medieval history professor was no other than Howard Adelson, a man equally familiar with Jewish history and the Holocaust, and, in addition, a descendant of Latvian Jews! He became my mentor and the supervisor of my dissertation, which eventually, somewhat rewritten and shorter, became the first volume of the trilogy, entitled *Journey Into Terror.*

The research necessary for such an undertaking took me to every country and every camp where Latvian Jews and/or deportees had suffered so much, had tried so hard to endure, and had, for the most part, become victims of the Germans and their all-too-willing collaborators.

When perusing the coldly official papers that recorded this suffering, I was dismayed by the misconceptions both groups had about each other. The main point, which none of us understood at the time of our arrival in Riga, was that in the eyes of the German authorities and their Latvian collaborators, we were all alike, that is, we were expendable and thus marked for murder.

Even at this late date, however, to my own sorrow, there are still misconceptions and therefore there is mistrust on both sides.

The small remnant of Latvian Jewry bears the burden of having witnessed foreign Jews taking over the very apartments from which their loved ones had been driven onto the streets and from there to the forest. To make matters worse, on December 10, 1941, while Latvian Jews were clearing these streets, collecting the bloodied bodies of those murdered in a last "clean-up" operation on December 9, for the purpose of taking them to the cemetery, they heard the ghetto's *Kommandant, Obersturmfuehrer* Kurt Krause tell the new arrivals from Cologne, "We brought you here to work. You speak German and this will make it easier for you to follow instructions!"

Not only the Latvian Jews believed what he said, but the bewildered newcomers did too. How could they think otherwise? The proof, or what they thought was proof, was all around them. It was on the blood-spattered walls of the apartments and staircases, the frozen food still on plates, clothing in disarray, sometimes even bodies of little children, overlooked or forgotten, and on the very street where they stood and listened to Krause, there was the cemetery, into which sad and silent men brought little sleds, heaped with bodies.

Neither group realized that up to that day, six transports from the Reich, containing over six thousand Jews, had already been murdered, five in Kovno, originally meant for Riga, and one that arrived on November 30 just in time to join the Latvian Jews as they stood in the Rumbuli Forest, awaiting their turn to be killed. There was no truth to the myth that the Latvian Jews had been killed to make room for the German Jews, but myths have a habit of lingering on.

No one, not even some of the Germans, knew what had transpired. There had been furious protest from some of the firms and military installations in Riga that had lost their employees when the Latvian Jews had been liquidated. Their letters reached Berlin, and SS *Obersturmbannfuehrer* Dr. Rudolf Lange was instructed to permit subsequent transports to remain alive for the time being "until such a time when a local workforce would be properly trained."

Later, in the fall of 1942, there was still more cause to suspect some German Jews of harming Latvian Jews. That was when the plans of an uprising were discovered and, after the murder of the Latvian Jewish police, the pride of the Latvian ghetto, German Jewish policemen were used to help in the subsequent apprehension of Latvian Jews and the search for weapons, leading to impassioned charges of betrayal.

Again, there is much evidence that it was a mishap that caused the discovery. Several young Latvian Jews, on their way to join the partisans in the forest, were apprehended and, rather than surrender, opened fire, killing several members of the patrol. The Germans were not only outraged, but perhaps even fearful. Their vengeance, which involved only the Latvian ghetto, was swift and furious. But the myth of betrayal persisted, despite proof to the contrary.

The deportees, on the other hand, had for years been programmed to believe that *Ostjuden,* by definition, were not quite up to par, on any level. Now, after the shock of relocation, they were confronted by a society of men, the sad remnants of a vibrant and distinguished community, and they felt inadequate. These were surely not the stereotypical Eastern European Jews they had heard about or known in earlier times. These were mainly younger men, for the most part rather handsome, dressed appropriately for the climate, and by no means totally destitute, at least when compared to the deportees.

Furthermore, as became clear very soon, while the Latvian Jews still had connections in Riga, as well as money, and therefore access to food, the new arrivals did not know the city, did not know the language, had been relieved of all their luggage, were not permitted to have money, and thus, were slowly starving. Their own young men were being sent to another camp, Salaspils, and their situation seemed hopeless. There was, in addition, the barbed wire fence separating the two ghettos, and I firmly believe that this was part of a well-designed plot by the Germans to keep the two groups apart, so as to increase their discomfort and prevent any cooperation between them. No matter, the Germans did not quite succeed, for the Latvian Jews, knowing of our hunger, made a concerted effort to give the children bread and milk.

How it must have hurt them . . . with their own children having been murdered only weeks earlier!

As time went by, just as in every other ghetto, there were love stories. Only very few Latvian Jewish women had survived, and the men were lonely. By the same token, many of the young German Jewish men had been killed in Salaspils. On most Sundays, the Latvian Jews received passes that enabled them to visit friends in the German ghetto and the young people enjoyed each other's company. It was evidently not enough, for despite some marriages that have endured to this day, there is still a gulf between the two communities, and I fear it cannot be bridged.

In my many years of research, I had to deal not only with human and social problems of these two groups that inhabited the ghetto, but also with numbers of victims. It was rather difficult to remain detached in the face of such an enormous calamity.

The extent of the tragedy in Latvia is an appalling one and not duplicated in other European countries. When the war between Germany and the Soviet Union started on June 22, 1941, there were eighty-three thousand Jews left in Latvia. Twelve thousand had been deported to Siberia just some weeks earlier. Of those twelve thousand and others who managed to flee in the last days, slightly more than four thousand survived. But of those eighty-three thousand who fell into German hands, no more than nine hundred saw liberation, among them some Jews from Kovno who had come to Riga in 1942 and had been added to the Latvian ghetto.

As far as the deportees are concerned, originally twenty-five thousand were to go to Riga. As I indicated earlier, the first five thousand went to Kovno instead, where the deportees from Munich, Berlin, and Frankfurt were murdered on November 25, 1941, and the deportees from Vienna and Breslau on November 29. Of the twenty thousand who reached Riga until February 10th, 1942 (my own transport), no more than eight hundred survived.

From February until December 1942, seventy more transports arrived. Most of them are marked ''Riga,'' but several are marked *''nach dem Osten.''* At the same time, some that were supposed to go to other killing centers and are still recorded as being destined for Auschwitz, or Theresienstadt, or Reval (Tallinn), ended up in Riga instead.

According to records at the *Institute fuer Zeitgeschichte* in Munich, there were only three instances when some young, strong men from such transports were selected for workplaces situated in other cities in Latvia, as for example Mitau (Jelgava). These exceptions concern three transports from Berlin, which left that city on September 5, 1942, September 14, 1942, and September 26, 1942. The last one of those three, which arrived in Riga on October 1, 1942, had originally been scheduled to go to Reval, but was instead shunted to Riga.

In early 1943, several transports of children, obviously from orphanages according to their metal tags that read *ohne Eltern* (without parents), arrived in Salaspils, where they were used for medical experiments. Also in 1943, transports from Kovno (Kaunas), Siauliai (Shavli), Vilno (Vilnius), and Libau (Liepaja) arrived at Kaiserwald and many of them found their last resting place in the forests around Riga, especially after the last selection on July 27, 1944.

It was in early summer of 1944 that five transports of Hungarian

Jewish women arrived from Auschwitz. Only a few hundred of them came to Kaiserwald; the others were sent directly to Dundaga and Poperwalen. Of the five thousand women, no more than three thousand were sent to Stutthof in early fall of 1944. The others found their graves in Latvia, for the most part right where they worked.

Figures alone cannot tell the story. All these were people; they lived and they loved and they laughed and they cried and they never, ever thought that they would suffer such a dreadful end. In the vast graveyard that is Latvia, they lie still, some of them turned into ashes in an effort to obscure the crime. It is our sacred duty to tell the world, to tell our children, and for them to tell their children how the world kept quiet while these innocents, for no other reason than being Jewish, were murdered in cold blood.

May the soil of Latvia rest lightly upon them and may their martyrdom never be forgotten. The authors of the vignettes contained in *Muted Voices* and *The Unfinished Road* have done their part, and at times it was very painful for them.

I, too, have tried my utmost to insure that the memory of all the victims, be they from Latvia, Germany, Austria, Czechoslovakia, or Hungary, be kept alive, and it is my fervent hope that future generations will do the same.

Bibliography

GENERAL READINGS

Books

Avotins, Evian, J. Dzirkalis and V. Petersons. *Daugavas Vanagi: Who Are They?* Riga: Latvian State Publishing House, 1963.

Dallin, Alexander. *German Rule in Russia, 1941–1945: A Study of Occupation Policies.* New York: St. Martin's Press, 1957.

Death Camp Salaspils. Riga: Publishing House Liesma, 1960.

Iwens, Sidney. *How Dark the Heavens: Fourteen Hundred Days in the Grip of the Nazi Terror.* New York: Shengold Publishers, 1990.

Katz, Josef. *One Who Came Back: The Diary of a Jewish Survivor.* Translated from German by Hilda Reach. New York: Herzl Press and Bergen-Belsen Memorial Press, 1973.

Kaufmann, Max. *Die Vernichtung der Juden Lettlands.* Munich: Deutscher Verlag, 1947.

Levinson, Isaac. *The Untold Story.* Johannesburg: Kayor Publishing House, 1958.

Maurina, Zenta. *Die Eisernen Riegel Zerbrechen.* Memmingen: Maximilian Dietrich Verlag, 1957.

Michelson, Frida. *I Survived Rumbuli.* Translated from Russian and edited by Wolf Goodman. New York: Holocaust Library, 1979.

Schneider, Gertrude. *Journey Into Terror: Story of the Riga Ghetto.* New York: Ark House, 1979.

————. *Muted Voices: Jewish Survivors of Latvia Remember.* New York: Philosophical Library, 1987.

Sherman, Hilde. *Zwischen Tag und Dunkel: Maedchenjahre im Ghetto.* Frankfurt am Main: Ullstein, 1984.

Silabriedis, J. and B. Arklans. *Political Refugees Unmasked.* Riga: Latvian State Publishing House, 1965.

The Jews in Latvia. Tel Aviv; D. Ben-Nun Press, 1971.

Wolff, Jeanette. *Sadismus oder Wahnsinn.* Dresden: Sachsenverlag, 1946.

Articles

Kaufmann, Max. "The Last Road of Professor Simon Dubnow." Translated and introduced by Professor George Schwab. Memorial booklet published in New York 1975.

Schneider, Gertrude. "The Jews of Riga." *Jewish Frontier* vol. 42, no. 3, pp. 15–20, 1975.

———. "Romance in the Ghetto." *Jewish Daily Forward* section B, October 19, 1980, pp. 1–10, 1980.

———. "Salaspils: The Story of an Extermination Camp." *The Jewish Press* vol. 35, no. 15, p. 24, 1985.

Seligman, Ruth. "Libau—The Town That Never Died." *Midstream* November 1986.

REFERENCES TO THE VARIOUS CHAPTERS

"The Unfinished Road," Gertrude Schneider

Grabowska, Janina. "Ewakuacja ladowa podobozow." In *Stutthof; Hitlerowski oboz koncentracyjny,* pp. 299–302. Warszawa: Wydawnictwo Interpress, 1988.

Orski, Marek. "Wykaz podobozow i wiekszych komand zewnetrznych KL Stutthof." In *Stutthof: Hitlerowski oboz koncentracyjny,* pp. 246–54. Warszawa: Wydawnictwo Interpress, 1988.

Piepka, Miroslaw. "Echa Wichrow Wojny." *Glos Wybrzeza,* nos. 37 and 38. Gdańsk, 1990.

Schneider, Gertrude. "Die Fahrt ins Grauen," *Der Neue Weg,* vol. 1, no. 5/6, pp. 3–10, 1946.

"The Jewish SS Officer," Alexander Levin

Huber, Hans Joachim. "Die Verhandlung des Dr. Fritz Scherwitz." *Echo der Woche,* Munich, November 3, 1949.

Kaufmann, Max. "Sich Selbst Ans Messer Geliefert." *Aufbau,* New York, June 11, 1948.

"The Death Sentence," Inge Berner

Paucker, Arnold. *Jüdischer Widerstand in Deutschland.* Berlin: Gedenkstaette Deutscher Widerstand, 1989.

Stern, Dr. Heinemann. *Warum Hassen Sie Uns Eigentlich?* Düsseldorf: Droste Verlag, 1970.

"The Last Jewish Knight of Vienna," Nina Ungar

Fontana, Oskar Maurus. *Wiener Schauspieler*. Austria: Amandus Edition, Wien, 1948.
Zwitter, Franci. "Österreichisch-jüdische Bühnen-schaffende," *Österreichisch-Jüdisches Geistes und Kulturleben*, Band 2, pp. 40–62. Wien: Literas Universitätsverlag, 1988.

"The Terrors of Dundaga," Abraham Shpungin

Vestermanis, Margers. "Das Seelager Dondangen—ein Modell für die geplante nazistische Neuordnung Europas." *Militärgeschichte*, vol. 2, pp. 145, 146. 1986.

"And I Almost Did Not Make It," Rita Wassermann

Weinzierl, Erika. *Zu wenig Gerechte: Österreicher und Judenverfolgung 1938–1945*, Graz, Wien, Köln: Verlag Styria, 1969.

"A Daughter Remembers," Eleonora Storch Schwab

Avriel, Ehud. *Open the Gates! A Personal Story of Illegal Immigration to Israel*. New York: Atheneum, 1975.
Fleming, Gerald. *Hitler and the Final Solution*. Berkeley and London: University of California Press, 1982.
Kersten, Felix. *The Memoirs of Doctor Felix Kersten*. New York: Doubleday and Co., 1947.
Kessel, Joseph. *The Man with the Miraculous Hands*. Translated from French by Helen Weaver and Leo Raditsa. New York: Farrar, Straus and Cudahy, 1961.
Koblik, Steven. *The Stones Cry Out: Sweden's Response to the Persecution of Jews, 1933–1945*. New York: Holocaust Library, 1988.
Laqueur, Walter. *The Terrible Secret: Suppression of the Truth About Hitler's "Final Solution."* New York and London: Penguin Books, 1982.
Penkower, Monty Noam. *The Jews Were Expendable: Free World Diplomacy and the Holocaust*. Urbana and Chicago: University of Illinois Press, 1983.
Toland, John. *Adolf Hitler*. New York: Ballantine Books, 1977.
"War Hero Dies in Sweden." *The Jewish Week*. New York, April 29, 1983.

Index of Names

Index of Places

About the Editor

GERTRUDE SCHNEIDER is Associate Placement Director and President of the Ph.D. Alumni Association at the City University of New York Graduate School. Dr. Schneider has lectured on the Holocaust at the University of Toronto, Oldenburg University, and the City University of New York Graduate School, among others. She is the editor of the *Latvian Jewish Courier* and is the author of *Journey Into Terror: The Story of the Riga Ghetto* and *Muted Voices: Jewish Survivors of Latvia Remember*. Her articles have appeared in such publications as the *Jewish Frontier, Jewish Social Studies,* the *Jewish Press,* and the *Daily Forward.* Dr. Schneider has been interviewed on a number of television programs including "60 Minutes" and has appeared in the film *Shoah.*